The Contexts of Acadian History, 1686–1784

NAOMI E.S. GRIFFITHS

The 1988 Winthrop Pickard Bell Lectures in Maritime Studies

Published for the Centre
for Canadian Studies
Mount Allison University
by
McGill-Queen's University Press
Montreal & Kingston • London • Buffalo

© Centre for Canadian Studies 1992
ISBN 0-7735-0883-x (cloth)
ISBN 0-7735-0886-4 (paper)
Reprinted in paperback 1993

Legal deposit first quarter 1992
Bibliothèque nationale du Québec

Printed in Canada on acid-free paper.

This book has been published with the help of a
grant from the Winthrop Pickard Bell Maritime
Studies Fund.

Canadian Cataloguing in Publication Data

Griffiths, N.E.S. (Naomi Elizabeth Saundaus), 1934–
    The contexts of Acadian history, 1686–1784
    (The Winthrop Pickard Bell lectures in maritime
    studies)
    Includes bibliographical references and index.
    ISBN 0-7735-0883-x (bound) –
    ISBN 0-7735-0886-4 (pbk.)
    1. Acadians – History. I. Mount Allison University.
    Centre for Canadian Studies. II. Title. III. Series.
    FC2041.G74 1992   971.5'00441   C91-090616-5
    F1037.G74 1992

This book was typeset by Typo Litho composition inc.
in 10/12 Palatino.

Poetry from *High Marsh Road* by Douglas Lochhead is
printed by permission of the author.

*For all those, loving and loved, who have had
a much tried faith in my ability to present
my ideas clearly — sooner or later*

Contents

Maps

Maps 1, 3, 5, 7, 8, and 9 were compiled by
Larry McCann and drafted by Cartographic
Services, Department of Geography, University
of Alberta. Map 3 is derived from A.H. Clark,
Acadia: The Geography of Nova Scotia to 1760.
Maps 5, 7, 8, and 9 are derived from Jean
Daigle and Robert LeBlanc, "Acadian
Deportation and Return," Plate 30, Historical
Atlas of Canada, vol. 1, ed. R.C. Harris.

Foreword

The Winthrop Pickard Bell Lectures are named in honour of a scholar who pioneered in the field of Maritime history and who was a generous benefactor of Mount Allison University. It was the wish of Winthrop Bell's family that a Chair of Maritime Studies be created in recognition of his many and varied contributions. Since 1977, over thirty distinguished scholars have visited the university for varying periods of time as the Bell Professor or as a Bell Lecturer. The lectures they presented to Mount Allison audiences in this capacity have been published as collections of essays or as monographs. The present volume, by Professor Naomi Griffiths of Carleton University, continues this tradition of scholarly enterprise.

Professor Griffiths held the Bell Chair at the Centre for Canadian Studies in the summer and fall of 1988, and delivered the lectures published here in late 1988 and early 1989. They represent her most recent thoughts on almost three decades of research on the Acadian people. Professor Griffiths first became interested in Acadian history while pursuing an MA degree at the University of New Brunswick. Her Ph.D. at the University of London focused on the Acadian deportation of the 1750s. Thereafter followed new research and a number of articles on various aspects of Acadian history. For her interpretation of the Acadian experience, she has been granted honorary degrees from the Université de Moncton and Collège Ste Anne.

Professor Griffiths' interest in understanding the Acadian experience has not waned. For the past several years, and since stepping down as Dean of Arts at Carleton, she has again gone in search of elusive archival materials in France, in Italy, in the United States, and, of course, in Canada. Her projected work is a large book, her "big" book, on the history of Acadians over several centuries. The Bell Lectures afforded Professor Griffiths the opportunity to conceptualize that study by writing about the contexts – social, economic, political, spatial, cultural – of Acadian history at several critical points in the emergence of this distinct society.

These essays reveal the nature of Professor Griffiths' scholarly quest. They display a sharp awareness of the need for an interdisciplinary approach. Geography, sociology, anthropology, and other disciplines inform the historical narrative and the interpretation of myriad facts and events. The lectures further demonstrate the importance of synthesis. Professor Griffiths' own archival research is very much in evidence, but so too is the work of other scholars. Finally, the lectures also reveal, most vividly, that understanding the Acadian identity requires an appreciation of the powerful story of the Acadian historical experience.

Naomi Griffiths graced the Bell Chair with honour and distinction. Her visit lingers in our minds: her support and wisdom; her infectious sense of humour; visiting classes; reading poetry at the Christmas party – all this and more were given in a wonderful spirit of sharing, of both scholarly pursuits and the experience of everyday life.

Larry McCann
Davidson Professor of
  Canadian Studies

Acknowledgments

The Winthrop Pickard Bell Chair in Maritime Studies is one of the most coveted awards for those of us working in the field. It gives to its fortunate holders a time of recollection in a place of wisdom. It enables the scholar to step back and consider how the particular problems and theories that are being confronted relate to the wider concerns of the community. It gives time to write without too many deadlines and yet provides, with the request to present one's ideas in a public forum, the necessity of explanation of what one is about to those who ought to be informed, not only one's colleagues but the wider community. My gratitude for this golden opportunity becomes greater as I find myself once more embroiled in the ordinary pursuits of a university faculty member. I owe more than I can express to the kindness and intelligence of all those I met during my brief stay in Sackville. I would like to single out for particular mention Larry McCann who is that rare being, a gentle, passionate and bloody-minded critic. For what is deemed valuable in what follows he bears a very large responsibility.

I should also like to take this opportunity to thank Carmen Bickerton, Barry Moody, George Rawlyk, and John Reid, who read the work in manuscript and whose suggestions were not only helpful but kindly put.

Finally, I would like to thank Carleton University and the SSHRC who have given generous aid towards the research costs incurred.

Introduction

One of the most difficult tasks that any scholar faces is the simple selection of topic. So much flows from this decision. For those of us in the Humanities and Social Sciences, much is revealed about our own preconceptions by the selection of the questions we find important and the ways in which we decide to treat the questions chosen. The need to be as explicit as possible about why one has pursued a certain line of research and why one considers certain sets of data evidence relevant to the questions one has proposed has become a common place for historians in the last twenty years.[1] Nevertheless, this requirement is something which still causes trouble among us because the myth still exists that well-written history implicitly makes plain the beliefs of the historian without the need for crude theoretical and methodological statements painstakingly expounded at the opening of a monograph.[2] I admit to a lingering belief that this proposition may still hold true for the most distinguished of my profession. I wish I could think myself dispensed from the soul-searching necessary to present my own epistemology. After all, what I want to talk about is far more interesting than my own mental universe. In the interests of clarity, however, I concede

1 See in particular David Hackett Fischer, *Historians' Fallacies: Towards a Logic of Historical Thought* (New York, 1970); T. Stoianovich, *French Historical Method: The Annales Paradigm* (Ithaca, NY, 1976); Francois Furet, *L'Atelier de l'histoire* (Paris, 1982); and Ian Craib, *Modern Social Theory from Parsons to Habermas* (New York, 1984).
2 See in particular Bernard Bailyn, "The Problems of a Working Historian: A Comment," in Sidney Hook, ed., *Philosophy and History* (New York, 1963), 93–4.

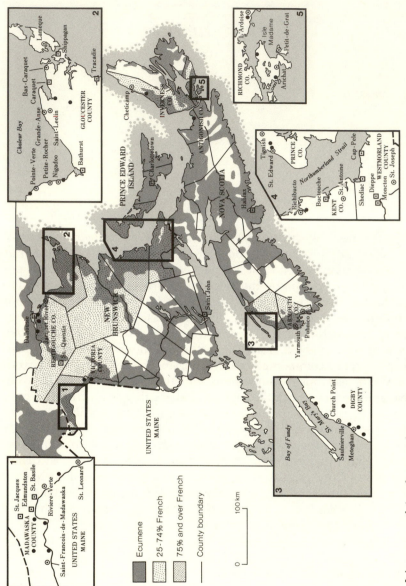

Major areas of Acadian settlement, c. 1986

Map 1 (Madawaska County area):
St. Jacques, Edmundston, St. Basile, Rivière-Verte, Saint-François-de-Madawaska, St. Leonard, MADAWASKA COUNTY, UNITED STATES, MAINE

Map 2 (Gloucester County area):
Chaleur Bay, Pointe-Verte, Petite-Rocher, Nigadoo, Bathurst, Grande-Anse, Saint-Léolin, Caraquet, Bas-Caraquet, Lamèque, Shippagan, Tracadie, GLOUCESTER COUNTY

Map 3 (Digby County area):
Bay of Fundy, St. Mary's Bay, Church Point, Saulnierville, Meteghan, DIGBY COUNTY

Map 4 (Kent / Westmorland area):
Tignish, St. Edward, PRINCE CO., Richibucto, Bouctouche, St-Antoine, KENT CO., Cap-Pelé, Shediac, Dieppe, Moncton, St. Joseph, WESTMORLAND COUNTY, Northumberland Strait

Map 5 (Richmond County area):
L'Ardoise, Isle Madame, Petit-de-Grat, Arichat, RICHMOND CO.

Main map labels:
UNITED STATES, MAINE, NEW BRUNSWICK, VICTORIA COUNTY, RESTIGOUCHE CO., Balmoral, Jacquet River, St. Quentin, Saint John, PRINCE EDWARD ISLAND, Charlottetown, Cheticamp, INVERNESS CO., ANTIGONISH CO., NOVA SCOTIA, Halifax, YARMOUTH CO., Yarmouth, Pubnico

Legend:
- Ecumene
- 25-74% French
- 75% and over French
- County boundary

0   100 km

the necessity of some general statement about what I want to achieve as an historian and how I think I can attain my aims.

My own life-long interest in Acadian history arises in part from an attraction to, and a knowledge of, present-day Acadian society. While there are a number of people who emphasize their Acadian heritage in Louisiana and in France, the centre of present-day twentieth-century Acadian society is to be found among the 300,000 French-speaking Canadians living in the Maritime provinces. In 1981 Statistics Canada reported that Acadians made up 5 percent of the population of Prince Edward Island, 4.2 percent of the population of Nova Scotia, and 33.6 percent of the population of New Brunswick.[3] I have known Acadian families throughout the Maritimes since 1953. I enjoy their folk singers, such as Edith Butler and Angele Arsenault, and am moved by their poets, especially by Herminegilde Chiasson and Leonard Forest.[4] Their novelists, not only their most famous author, Antonine Maillet, whose novel *Pélagie-la-Charette* received the Prix Goncourt in 1975; but others, such as Laurier Melanson,[5] record worlds that have a ring of truth for me. Acadian dance and theatre, painting and sculpture, folk art, and cooking,[6] are all to my taste. Above all, the countryside in which Acadians live and work is, to my eyes, one of great loveliness. I like the architecture of their mid-twentieth-century churches and their cathedrals. The fact that, in the cathedral in Edmundston, the stained glass windows have pictures of those who paid for them in their modern business suits delights me. Today's Acadian community is to be found in some of Canada's most beautiful settings, the sand dune beaches of Buctouche, the wooded river valleys of Madawaska country, the sea shore between Shediac and Cap-Pele, and the many enclaves in Nova Scotia and Prince Edward Island.

If part of my interest in things Acadian springs from knowledge of the present-day community, another part comes from an intel-

3 These figures are based on those who report French as a mother tongue and do not include those who consider themselves Acadian but who no longer claim French as a language spoken in the home.
4 A good introduction to Acadian writing is through the publications of Les Editions de l'Acadie, in particular the work edited by Marguerite Maillet, Gerard Leblanc, and Bernard Emont, *Anthologie de textes litteraires Acadiens 1606–1975* (Moncton, 1979).
5 *Zelika a Cochon Vert* (Montreal, 1981).
6 For those unfortunate enough not to be able to taste Acadian cooking *sur place*, a good introduction is provided by Marielle Boudreau and Melvin Gallant, *Le Guide de la Cuisine Traditionnelle* (Moncton, 1980).

lectual curiosity about why any people think themselves members of a particular community, and the ways in which this identification is important for them. My introduction to people who considered themselves as "Acadian" came even before I emigrated to Canada in 1956. In 1953 I met students from New Brunswick at London University, students who spoke French as a mother tongue, and who saw themselves as having a Canadian identity that was coloured by an additional heritage. It was from them I learnt that the history of Acadia reached back to the seventeenth century and that it was a history of drama, complexity, and endurance. In their telling, it was the history of a people who had never had political independence but had evolved a strong sense of a unique identity. It was a history that was, apparently, dominated by events in the eighteenth century, a deportation of the majority of the community in 1755 from ancestral lands, an incident of the world war being waged at that time between England and France. I was unclear, in the 1950s, as to how, or how much of, a community deported returned, but I was very clear that an Acadian identity was something held as strongly by my new acquaintances as a Welsh identity by my father's family.

My formal study of the Acadians began in 1956 when I went to the University of New Brunswick to work with Dr. A.G. Bailey. Under his guidance, and with the help of Father René Baudry at what was then Collège St Joseph of Memramcook, I began to try to understand what the deportation of 1755 had actually involved and also what historians had thought the deportation had involved. Since then, Acadian history has been for me an avocation as much as a professional concern.

Fundamentally, much of my interest is in questions of what is now called ethnohistory, a discipline Bruce Trigger considers that A.G. Bailey founded with his work *The Conflict of European and Eastern Algonkian Cultures, 1504–1700: A Study in Canadian Civilization.*[7] What elements are the building blocks of a sense of community identity? How do human communities produce a sense of "national" identity, which is then carried through the years and used both as a powerful political and social tool? How enduring are the elements which are brought together in this sense of uniqueness? How do the ideas and beliefs of one generation retain importance for those who come after, people whose problems and difficulties are very different from those confronted by their ancestors?

7 Trigger's comment appears in *Natives and Newcomers: Canada's "Heroic Age" Reconsidered* (Montreal, 1985), 45.

From this standpoint, Acadian history is an almost perfect subject of enquiry, for the Acadian community has an obvious beginning and a complex and intricate development. There were no Acadians before the middle of the seventeenth century; that is to say, until then there were no people whose community identification of themselves was "Acadian." The Acadian community was built by migrants from Europe to North America, migrants whose European backgrounds were by no means homogenous. As will be shown in chapter 1, the explanation of Acadian distinctiveness does not lie in the transference of an identity already forged in Europe.

So in tackling questions about the roots of Acadian identity, I have been brought to study a number of the more general questions about the history of the migration of Europeans to North America, a phenomenon that is rooted in the seventeenth century. During this century the North Atlantic became not merely the ocean for Europeans to sail and fish, but their sea and passageway – their route for travelling to new lands.[8] Bernard Bailyn views the trans-Atlantic migration from Europe, which began in earnest after 1600, as more responsible than anything else for the transformation of the life of the world over the last three centuries.[9] It was, in his words,

the movement of people outward from their original centres of habitation – the centrifugal *Volkerwanderungen* that involved an untraceable multitude of local, small-scale exoduses and colonizations, the continuous creation of new frontiers and ever-widening circumferences, the complex intermingling of peoples in the expanding border areas, and in the end the massive transfer to the Western Hemisphere of people, from Africa, from the European mainland, and above all from the Anglo-Celtic offshore islands of Europe, culminating in what Bismarck called "the decisive fact in the modern world," the peopling of the North American continent.

The history of Acadian development is a small part of this immense movement. Its study has led me to elucidate the various ways in which Europe reached across the Atlantic during the seventeenth and eighteenth centuries and the ways in which newcomers from Europe established their communities in what were, to the migrants, not only new but very unusual circumstances. These endeavours

8 For a classic exposition of these ideas see J.H. Parry, *The Discovery of the Sea* (Berkeley, 1981), 184–233.

9 Bernard Bailyn, *The Peopling of North America: An Introduction* (New York, 1988), 4.

require both a knowledge of present historical debate about the most important characteristics of Europe during the period in question and of the equally intricate arguments over the situation of Amerindian life during the same period. The obvious guide for me through the maze of ideas and information, both about European peoples and their ideologies during this time and about the lives and beliefs of the Micmac and Malecite peoples (the Amerindians with whom the Acadians are most closely linked), was the attempt to construct a critical narrative of Acadian history.

By making the structure of my enquiry a very traditional historical task – establishing a factual account verifiable by any scholar willing to retrace the archival research presented – the most complex questions concerning the development of a distinct identity of the Acadian communities are given a stable frame of reference. My first task has been to ensure that the events of Acadian history are clear. Who commanded what expeditions to Acadie? When? Under what conditions? With what European authority as backing? To what effect, in terms of land claimed and held, was commerce established? What are the significant points, in time, of the growth and development of the colony? When did it become self-supporting in terms of food? When was its population pool large enough to produce a growing Euroamerican population without additional migration? A great deal has been written in both French and English about the political and diplomatic events of Acadian history. A significant number of historians have had as an ambition a definitive narrative account of Acadian history.[10] However, no work published in either language has connected Acadian experience with the heritage of ideas and knowledge brought by the migrants to the new lands.

It is in this sphere that I wish to build upon my own archival work about the events of Acadian development. I want to explore what can be known of the characteristics of those who sailed from Europe and whose descendants called themselves Acadian. By this I mean, what was the family background of those who went? What customs did their childhood experiences provide them for coping with new environments and new companions? What political and religious institutions had influenced them enabling them to set out for a life in an unfamiliar environment? While it is difficult to unearth the biography of each individual who left for the New World, there is

10 Classics of this line of inquiry are R. Rumilly, *Histoire des Acadiens*,
    2 vols. (Montreal, 1955); and J.B. Brebner, *New England's Outpost* (New
    York, 1927).

considerable information about the areas from which the migrants came at the time of their departure. The records of the Atlantic ports of France and England, linked to the genealogical work of the Centre d'études acadiennes about those who survived in the settlements established, can be used to present ideas about the areas of Europe that were the starting points for the travellers. During the last thirty years the scholarship about seventeenth-century France has been prodigious. The recreation of the mind-set and material culture of the average migrant to Acadie can now be attempted.

An account of the sorts of people who came to settle the lands that, between 1628 and 1763, were referred to in international treaties as "Acadia or Nova Scotia" is only part of what must be given. A crucial part of the story of Acadian life during the years of the settlement and development of new communities is the impact on the nascent Acadian society not only of France and England, but also of their increasing interest in their North American empires. The Atlantic connected North America and Europe quite as much as it separated the two continents. It is not possible to present the European heritage of Acadia as a single sketch pinned to a particular point in time. Communication of changing European ideas, and the impact of changing European policies altered the circumstances of Acadian development over the decades. The transformation of the ideological universes of France and England between 1550 and 1760 affected those, during these centuries, who were engaged in trans-Atlantic migration. It may be that all that I can achieve is to show how complex this relationship was for the migrant, for the colony, and for the officials of the metropolitan powers engaged in developing dreams of Empire. Even this achievement, however, would help to destroy some of the dangerous myths about the unchanging historical sameness of English and French national characteristics.

The development of Acadian society by the migrants and their descendants poses as many complex problems to be explored as does the European aspect of its life. But one of the great advantages for students of the Acadian community during the seventeenth and eighteenth centuries is the fact that, relatively speaking, it was such a small community. By 1710, the American settlements had more than 350,000 people and New France, about 16,000, but Acadia had no more than 2,000. The smallness of sample is coupled with a considerable richness of primary documentation: a wealth of official church records, official censuses, and even a few personal reminiscences. This has emboldened me to speculate on what can be said about the relationship between the experience of the individual and the nature of social change; in particular, to ask questions about family structure and social needs, and about the mediating role played by the family in both maintaining and creating social norms. It has made me ask questions about the intersection of the life-course structure and family cycles, and about the tension between social needs, community demands, and individual ambitions.

My ambition is to render the history of a very small group of humanity intelligible from the view-point both of the larger conglomerations of people and from the stance of the individual. The Winthrop Pickard Bell lectures provided me with a magnificent opportunity to outline in some detail and for four specific periods the intricate nature of the history I wish to write. Of course, the judgment that a particular number of years is to be considered as a formative era is as subjective a decision as the selection of a particular fact as one having major significance. For me, the 1680s, the years during which migration from France to Acadie became an addition to a population rather than the founding of that colony, are a reasonable starting place for Acadian history. Like most historians I really want to begin with what Professor Humphries of the University of British Columbia has defined as the logical place for all historians, the time when "the Earth was slowly cooling." An examination of the 1680s, however, allows an examination of the mix of European heritage and North American environment in the early years of Acadian life. Above all, the history of these years provides an opportunity to show the way in which seventeenth-century national ideologies were quite different, both in importance and in content, from their counterparts in the nineteenth and twentieth centuries. The second era chosen, the 1730s, is an era in which one can see an Acadian community flourishing, economically, politically, socially, and culturally. Writing elsewhere I have described it as the Golden Age of Acadia.[11] It is important to understand what happened in these years not only because of what Acadian life was during this period but also because these years were the basis of the Acadian vision of life before the deportation of 1755. They were the years that would be imagined by Longfellow in his poem. They were years that would be remembered as a time of innocence and plenty, the formative years of the character of the Acadian community. The third and fourth periods were almost self-defined: they encompass the years leading up to the deportation, and the immediate period of exile. Questions about the why and how of the

11 N.E.S. Griffiths "The Golden Age: Acadian Life, 1713–1748," *Histoire sociale–Social History*, vol. 17, no. 33 (mai–May, 1984): 24–34.

deportation may never find answers agreeable to all. In these lectures I tried to present what I believe are the most important questions to discuss and an overview of the evidence which must be considered.

This present work represents a limited development of those lectures. My hope is that before too long I will be able to complete a major work which will gain its internal consistency from the presentation of the world of those whose lives made up that collectivity of Acadia. What makes Acadian history of such vital interest to me is that it is about people who decided to identify their sense of community by the word "Acadia," creating a people where none had been before. How did this occur? What were the important points in the evolution of the society of migrants into a polity, a polity which has endured in spite of extraordinary trials? I hope that the reader will find the beginnings of answers in what follows.

Abbreviations

The following abbreviations or shortened references are used in the notes.

AC   Archives des Colonies (Paris)
DCB *Dictionary of Canadian Biography*. Edited by George Brown et al. In progress. Toronto, 1965–   .
NA   National Archives of Canada
PANS Public Archives of Nova Scotia

The Contexts of Acadian History, 1686–1784

CHAPTER ONE

The 1680s: Settlement Achieved

In 1604, the first formal European attempt was made to settle the lands which would be known as "Acadia or Nova Scotia" in international treaties from 1628 to 1763. The year before, 1603, the then King of France, Henri IV, commissioned Pierre du Gast, Sieur de Monts, as his Vice-Roy and Captain-General "on sea and on land in La Cadie, Canada and other parts of New France between 40 and 60°," and bid him administer the settlement of the territories thus designated.[1] The next eighty years saw a slow and often bitter struggle to establish a new community of people, mostly from France but some from England, on the lands today called Nova Scotia. It was not until the late 1680s that an economically self-sustaining and demographically self-generating colony could be found there. By 1689, Acadie had approximately one thousand Euroamerican inhabitants and two or three thousand Amerindians, mostly Micmacs.[2] The main language of the settlers was French, but English was understood by many. The religious affiliation was Catholic, but it was not an intolerant community, and the existence of Protestant belief in the society must be considered.

1 "Commission of de Monts as Lieut. Gen. in Acadie, 29 January 1605," AC, C–11–A.I, 58 ff. Printed in Marc Lescarbot, *The History of New France*, edited by W.L. Grant et H.P. Biggar, (Toronto: Champlain Society, 1911), 2: 211–26.

2 The figures for those of European descent are estimates by A.H. Clark, *Acadia: The Geography of Nova Scotia* (Madison, 1968), 123. He has cited the numerous censuses that were made during the 1680s. See also M. Roy, "Peuplement et croissance demographique," in Jean Daigle, ed., *Les Acadiens des Maritimes* (Moncton, 1980), 144.

While an Acadian identity was still in the making at the close of the 1680s, one can already see many of the characteristics that were to be important later. In these early years of struggle, the community developed attitudes towards external authority, whether secular or religious; to the possession and development of land, to the Micmac and Malecite peoples; and to the larger colonial settlements of New France and New England. All would develop into distinctively Acadian positions about such matters in the early eighteenth century. The emerging Acadian identity was created from the daily rhythm of activity and the changing relationships between the migrant and the new world. Still, the continuing power of things European was ever present.

As David Quinn has repeatedly emphasized, "It is a truism, but one we must not lose sight of, that the European colonies in the Americas sprang out of the distinct historical experiences and traditions of England, France and Spain."[3] Above all else, it was the political life of the new societies that was dominated by Europe. First, the policies of the metropolises had undeniable consequences for the colonies, if not always in the ways intended. Second, the political thought of Europe – based on ideas about state authority and institutions, about religious beliefs and organizations, and about legal rights and the processes of governance – provided the starting-place for the political rhetoric of the new societies. If both European state policies and European political theories were complex, almost enigmatic resources for the migrants, they were, nevertheless, inescapable bequests to those who founded the new polities in North America.

Nor, was the European heritage of the migrant confined to some single political event or unchanging political theory. As far as practical and theoretical policies were concerned, communication across the Atlantic between the metropolitans and the colonists never ceased, even though the pace and importance of such communications waxed and waned. Similarly, in matters of the social and cultural developments of the colonies, the European influence was of continual, if fluctuating, importance.

Debate has been vigorous about the relative importance of European heritage and North American resources in shaping the new

---

3 David B. Quinn, "Colonies in the Beginning: Examples from North America," in Stanley H. Palmer and Dennis Reinhartz, eds., *Essays on the History of North American Discovery and Exploration*, Walter Prescott Webb Memorial Lectures (Austin, 1988), 10.

societies.[4] Yet, for Acadia during the seventeenth century, as for most other European colonies in North America at that time, the importance of the European component of life was just as great as that of the North American elements. At any particular time one or other influence might be paramount but at no time was either influence completely absent from the political life and concerns of the colonists. Further, the colonists were not some unchanging element in a closed system, any more than France and England were static components of a trans-Atlantic world. Rather, the North American environment and European influence, themselves in the process of development, had a changing impact upon settlements experiencing their own internal growth.

The decades which saw France move from the chaotic reign of Louis XIII to the war-torn bitterness of Louis XIV's final years, and England experience the collapse of Stuart government, also saw major changes in conditions in North America. The devastation of the Amerindians, which had begun in the sixteenth century, slowed but did not cease during the seventeenth century; and the impact of the fur trade upon North American ecology became inescapably noticeable during these same decades.[5] These alterations meant that Acadia was subject to a changing variety of external influences while simultaneously coping with internal development. The society in the small town of Port Royal at the end of the 1680s was much different from that of the first fort, Port Royal, in 1605.

4 The concept of the frontier lands of North America as the most important factor in the moulding of new societies was first put forward by F.J. Turner in "The Significance of the Frontier in American History," *Annual Report of the American Historical Association for the Year 1893* (Washington, DC, 1894), 199–277. Those who stressed the European heritage found an articulate spokesman in Louis Hartz, *The Founding of New Societies: Studies in the Social History of the United States, Latin America, South Africa, Canada and Australia* (New York, 1964). For an insightful analysis of both arguments see the Canadian Historical Association presidential address by S.F. Wise, "Liberal Consensus or Ideological Background: Some Reflections on the Hartz Thesis," *Historical Papers/ Communications Historiques* (Ottawa, 1974), 1–15.

5 On the question of Amerindian demography see in particular James Axtell, *The European and the Indian: Essays in the Ethnohistory of North America* (New York, 1981) and *The Invasion Within: The Contest of Cultures in Colonial North America* (New York, 1985). On the question of ecology see Calvin Martin, *Keepers of the Game: Indian-Animal Relations and the Fur Trade* (Los Angeles, 1978).

The question of the boundaries of "Acadia or Nova Scotia" clearly reflects at least one source of the tension between European and American realities – a tension that would lead the Acadians to formulate a policy of neutrality. This question involved both the ambitions of European statesmen and the realities of North American geography. Exact knowledge of North American geography was obviously not part of the mental landscape of seventeenth-century European statesmen and bureaucrats. As a result, the claims and counter-claims of European powers to the vast lands now opening up were bedevilled by vague and inexact information about the extent and position of what was being argued about.[6] The North American policies of England and France towards "Acadia or Nova Scotia" were largely shaped by territorial ambitions for unknown lands, ambitions which had little to do with existing European settlement in North America. Further, as the dual name implies, disputes between these European powers were not only about where the limits of the Acadian territory should be drawn but also, frequently enough, about whose colony it was that the Acadians inhabited.

Claim and counter-claim to the eventual lands of the Acadians began almost as early as the first attempt at settlement. After all, while one can talk, as K.R. Andrews does, of the "invasion of America" as "a European movement,"[7] it is important to remember that it was an invasion that carried European rivalries across the Atlantic. When Acadia was first made the object of French settlement ambitions, at the same time the English were making a bid for a place in the Gulf of St Lawrence and exploring the coast of what would be New England.[8] Not only were explorers, traders, missionaries, and the occasional would-be settler from both countries investigating much the same part of the world but the official claims of their governments for that same territory were extensive, vague, and

6 On the debate over the authority argued in Europe for such claims see Olive Patricia Dickason, "Old World Law, New World Peoples and Concepts of Sovereignty," in Palmer and Reinhartz, eds., *Essays*, 52–78. Some of the ideas elaborated in this essay are in L.C. Green and Olive P. Dickason, *The Law of Nations and the New World* (Edmonton, 1989).

7 Kenneth R. Andrews, *Trade, Plunder and Settlement: Maritime Enterprise and the Genesis of the British Empire, 1480–1630* (Cambridge, 1984), 304.

8 David B. Quinn, *England and the Discovery of America, 1481–1620* (New York, 1974), 311–63.

often conflicting. The grant of land given to de Monts in 1603 was as expansive as it was vague.[9] Eighteen years later, in 1621, the Scots proved not much more precise. In that year, James I of England and VI of Scotland initiated colonial development in the same general region, named for his purposes Nova Scotia or New Scotland,[10] and the official documents handed to his deputy, Sir William Alexander, later Viscount Stirling, maintained rights over much the same territory with similarly inaccurate largesse. It was claimed at the time that the grant was the better-made, being delimited by landmark rather than by latitude. Sir William Alexander wrote "that mine be the first National Patent that was ever clearly bounded within America by particular limits upon the Earth."[11] In fact, setting the boundaries as the St Croix and St Lawrence rivers produced a jurisdiction just as unworkable as any resulting from claims based on degrees of latitude. As the seventeenth century developed and European colonization established other major settlements on either side of Acadian territory, all with boundaries as vague, extraordinarily complex disputes arose over the limits of the lands claimed.

No matter who claimed "Acadia or Nova Scotia," throughout most of the period from 1604 and 1763 it was considered to be centered on present-day Nova Scotia and southern New Brunswick, with some right to a part of north-eastern Maine and south-eastern Quebec. At the opening of the seventeenth century, this was an area of minor economic and social ambition for both England and France. But by the 1680s, the area had gained a major significance for both these powers, mostly because of its political geography. "Acadia or Nova Scotia" had become the meeting point of much greater territories for which these two powers did have major, far-reaching, and conflicting designs. It was obvious that the homeland of the Acadians was one of the most important stretches of the border between the burgeoning entities of New England and New France.

Further, "Acadia or Nova Scotia" was no different than any other borderland between greater powers. It was ruled first by one, then

9 "Patent, Nov. 8th, 1603," AC, C–11–A.I., 78 ff.; "Commission of de Monts as Lieut. Gen. in Acadie, Jan. 29, 1605," AC, C–11–A.I., 58 ff., both in Grant and Biggar, *The History of New France*, 2: 211–26.

10 The best modern account of these efforts is by John Reid, *Acadia, Maine and New Scotland: Marginal Colonies in the Seventeenth Century* (Toronto, 1981).

11 On the political ramifications of the Scottish claims see Reid, *Acadia*, particularly 24–5.

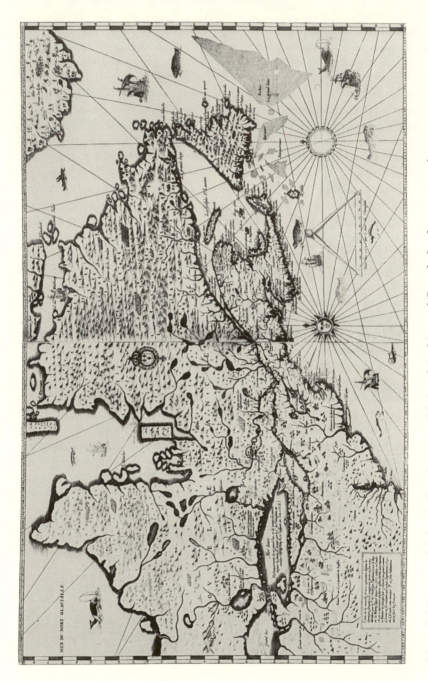

Champlain's map of Atlantic Canada, 1632. (National Archives of Canada [NA], NMC 51970)

by the other. The importance of Scottish and English control of the colony in the seventeenth century has too often been, if not overlooked, much underestimated.[12] Yet, as well as brief years of Scottish control at the close of the 1620s, there was an extended period from 1654 to 1670 when the colony was governed through London and Boston. A.H. Clark has referred to these years as an "interregnum,"[13] but they were of crucial importance for Acadian life. They were, in fact, a turning-point for Acadian attitudes towards religion, political theories, and land ownership. The communication links between the Acadians and "les Bostonnais" unfolded at this time, in such a way as to allow the former to consider the latter, in Jean Daigle's words, "nos amis les ennemis."[14] They were years when the Acadians became a border people, such as the Basques, rather than simply people on a border, such as the Lowland Scots.

By the 1680s the settlements of "Acadia or Nova Scotia" had known both French and English government and had experienced the impact of the ambitions both of New England and New France as well. France had always paid more sustained attention to Acadia than had England. After almost three generations of effort the colony only barely existed. While Acadia was most often recognized as a French possession between 1604 and 1713, it never received major subsidies for its development over any extended period from any French government. Its place in the affairs of the French state was minimal, of even less account than that of Quebec.[15]

It is important to be clear about the place of colonial development in the policies of the emerging nation-states of Europe during the seventeenth century. It is easy enough to pre-date national concerns of the nineteenth and twentieth centuries and to find more than the shadows of their being in earlier times. While some aspects of nationalist ideologies were slowly emerging in seventeenth-century Europe, the circumstances needed to foster anything recognisable

12 Two major exceptions to this are the work of George Rawlyk, *Nova Scotia's Massachusetts: A Study of Massachusetts-Nova Scotia Relations, 1630 to 1784* (Montreal, 1978); and Reid, *Acadia*.

13 Clark, *Acadia*, 107–8.

14 Jean Daigle, *Nos amis les ennemis: relations commerciales de l'Acadie avec le Massachusetts, 1670–1711*, PHD dissertation, University of Maine, 1975.

15 Peter N. Moogk, "Reluctant Exiles: Emigrants from France in Canada before 1760," *The William and Mary Quarterly* 46 (1989): 463–505.

as modern nationalism did not yet exist.[16] French migration across the Atlantic in the seventeenth century was not the westward sweep of nation. As Peter Moogk has noted, "It would be anachronistic to refer to Bretons, Basques, Flemings, Alsatians, Provencaux and speakers of French dialects as 'the French people.'"[17] The migration was instead a slow and cautious extension of French state policies and the tentative adventures of small groups.[18]

In the context of seventeenth-century European political development, French and English policies towards Acadia were both shaped by two factors, one political and one economic. First, the nature and interests of state governments in seventeenth-century Europe were still linked, primarily, to the fortunes of their rulers, and to the families of their rulers. Much of political life was still dominated by the needs of the monarch to guard his hereditary right and secure such rights for his descendants. This meant that internal policies of order, aimed at ensuring not only the security of the realm but the primacy of the house of the monarch, were the major and dominant concern of those who ruled. Throughout most of the seventeenth century, both France and England were subject to a series of civil disturbances; England with the concentrated agony of the Civil War, France with the fighting of the Fronde and the consequences of the Revocation of the Edict of Nantes. For those who governed both countries the priority for all resources, intellectual as well as economic, was the domestic life of the realm.

Second, one needs to bear in mind that the economic value of settlement colonies such as New England, and New France and Acadie, was of low priority for much of the seventeenth century. Trade in fur and fish did not require year-round settlement for their initial prosecution, although both could be said to benefit from such developments in the long run. There were many arguments in France in the first half of the seventeenth century against allowing

16 See in particular E. Gellner, "Nationalism and the Two Forms of Cohesion in Complex Societies," in Gellner, *Culture, Identity and Politics* (Cambridge, 1978), 15.

17 Moogk, "Reluctant Exiles," 504.

18 The work by L.P. Choquette, "French Emigration to Canada in the Seventeenth and Eighteenth Centuries" PHD dissertation, Harvard University, 1988, is the most comprehensive analysis to date of this subject.

settlement, and the official proscription by the English of year-round establishments in Newfoundland is well known.[19]

Yet, this said, it is also clear that the concept of colonies played a major role in the formulation of policy by both France and England from the late sixteenth century onward. As John Reid has pointed out, the lure of the colonial enterprise arose, to some extent, from a desire to emulate the achievements of Spain in the sixteenth century and to establish "extensive areas of colonization which would bring national prestige and personal prestige to those directly involved."[20] There was a constant hope of direct, major economic benefits for the European base, whether from large finds of gold and other precious metals and stones or through some other obvious and visible source of wealth. Should the enterprise in question not yield these immediate riches, then its value in the eyes of the European governments declined precipitously. And with this decline came neglect, except when control of the colony could be seen either as the key to dominance elsewhere, or as a useful bargaining chip in the general play of international politics, or as providing a minor, but real, accretion of status at a time when such an addition would be valuable.

In 1686 events persuaded Louis XIV and his ministers that Acadia represented a conjunction of just these elements. This was a year when both England and France were to reap the first sheaves of an increasingly bitter harvest. In England James II had just come to the throne, determined to restore the country to Catholicism and a proper understanding of the rights of kings. The year before in France, Louis XIV had revoked the Edict of Nantes, thereby ending all pretence at religious toleration within his jurisdiction. In 1686 both kings understood that the debatable consequences of their actions demanded an organization of policies that would successfully underline the wisdom of their exploits. Both wished to resolve all external matters so that their domestic policies would be the more readily tolerated and could be given full attention. One of the results of this mutual stock-taking was the attempt to settle the questions

19 C. Grant Head, *Eighteenth Century Newfoundland: A Geographic Perspective* (Toronto, 1976); and L. Codignola, *The Coldest Harbour of the Land: Simon Stock and Lord Baltimore's Colony in Newfoundland, 1621–1649* (Kingston & Montreal 1988).
20 Reid, *Acadia*, xiv.

of their North American interests in the treaty of neutrality signed at Whitehall on 16 November 1686.

It was a treaty based firmly upon the European-centred belief that colonies were extensions of the monarchs' realms. It was conceived with little or no understanding that the colonies had political ambitions of their own and that such ambitions for their futures were different from those proposed for them by the metropolitans.[21] It showed little or no understanding of the geography or economics of either Massachusetts or Acadia, or of the web of interdependence which by now linked the two colonies. The clauses within it that dealt specifically with North American matters were such as to so disadvantage one side or the other that their observance was unlikely from the start.

George Rawlyk has noted about one such clause: "What the treaty specifically prohibited was the drying of fish on Nova Scotia soil by Massachusetts fishermen, a drastic measure which, if enforced, would significantly affect the entire Massachusetts economy."[22] Leaving aside the question of how such a provision could be enforced, given the geography of the coastlines involved and the technology of the naval forces available, those who wrote this clause clearly had no appreciation of the way in which the Atlantic fishery was pursued by those in the colonies, nor of the place of that fishery in the economies of Massachusetts and Acadia.

But these matters were of minor importance to the diplomats in Europe. The most important provision of the treaty in their view, was at the same time the least important for the North American colonist. This was the stipulation, that even though the two countries might be at war in Europe, "their colonies in America should continue in peace and neutrality."[23] One implicit assumption here is that warfare between the colonies in North America would be subject to close control from the other side of the Atlantic. Remember that

---

21 London's colonial policy is effectively analyzed by W.A. Speck, "The International and Imperial Context," in Jack P. Greene and J. R. Pole, eds., *Colonial British America: Essays in the New History of the Modern Early Era* (Baltimore, 1984), 384–407, esp. 395; and that of Versailles by C.W. Cole, *Colbert and a Century of French Mercantilism*, 2 vols. (Connecticut, 1964), 2: 1–131.

22 Rawlyk, *Nova Scotia's Massachusetts*, 49.

23 The treaty is printed in *Edits, ordonnances royaux, declarations et arrets du Conseil d'Etat du roi concernant le Canada*, 3 vols. (Quebec, 1803), 1: 258.

this was a time when the speed of communication across the ocean depended upon technologies particularly subject to the vagaries of weather. The fastest crossing in the most favourable of circumstances by the best of the tall ships was forty-nine days.[24] Further, this is only for the one-way sea passage, port to port. Thus, very great deal could take place in the usual time it took to send a letter from a colonial outpost to the counsels of state and receive a reply. Transaction very rarely took less than five months and this was when a missive was answered promptly, something that rarely happened.

In other words, despite all the inadequacies of seventeenth-century communication technology, and in spite of the limits of European knowledge about conditions on the periphery of their empires, the metropolitan authorities both of France and England shaped their policies in the belief that what was decided in London and Paris would be accepted and carried out in colonial outposts. It was a belief which rested, in part, on the undoubted authority of metropolitan authorities to appoint colonial officials. The method of appointment was as effective and the quality of the men named as varied as in appointments made to similar positions in the mother country. Sometimes competence was discovered and rewarded; sometimes influence meant patronage of the corrupt and incompetent. As far as France was concerned, the personal authority of the monarch was the determining factor in the distribution of official commissions.

What all this meant for Acadia, and even for other French colonies, was a very haphazard and arbitrary metropolitan rule. Acadian affairs were never as significant to the French as they were to the Acadians. While those appointed to serve in the colony might occasionally be chosen as competent to carry out some particular policy of the metropolitan authorities, more often than not those sent were men who had achieved appointment through influence rather than merit.

For example, on 10 April 1684, Francoise Perrot, whose activities of smuggling and general craftiness had caused his dismissal as the Governor of Montreal, was appointed as Governor of Acadia.[25] He carried on in much the same spirit from Port Royal, the major Acadian settlement, as he had done on the St Lawrence. He sent linen

24 Gilles Proulx, *Between France and New France: Life Aboard the Tall Sailing Ships* (Charlottetown, 1984), 57.

25 On this engaging scamp see W. J. Eccles, "Francoise-Marie Perrot," *DCB*, 1: 540–2.

and wine direct to Boston and continued measuring out "even in his own house, under the eyes of the foreigners, his pints and half pints of brandy."[26] His career in Acadia was brought to an end in 1687. This was less because of French concern about the damage his corrupt incompetency would cause the colony than because, as has already been suggested, statesmen in Europe then turned a greater amount of their attention than usual to the affairs of New England and New France, and France saw Acadia as a significant pawn in international politics.

The arbitrary but effective power that Louis XIV could exercise was shown in the appointment of Perrot's successor. Having decided that the colony could play a useful part in his grand designs, Louis himself attended to the question of the colony's governor. He did not merely confirm a proposed candidate but presided over a discussion of possible choices. Louis XIV, as an absolute monarch and the necessary, directing intelligence of his state, was at this point in time coping with the domestic turmoil that was stemming from the Revocation of the Edict of Nantes and the foreign affairs which were the prelude to what many have called the first world war.[27] Yet the question of French territorial sovereignty around the Bay of Fundy became a matter of considerable interest and attention for him. When the small conclave of ministers met with Louis XIV, even as the problems of disaffection and distress within the realm were pressing for discussion and as matters of European diplomatic policy jostled one another for their meagre allotment of mind and time, the appointment of officials for Acadia was decided and the necessary letters of instruction for those involved in the colony's affairs were brought forth for his signature.

It is perhaps difficult to visualize in late twentieth-century Canada, with telephones and word-processors and an extensive civil service, how the conduct of government was carried on in 1686. Those engaged in running the state evolved their strategies and tactics in a world where the transmission of information across space was subject to the vagaries of weather and the speed of horse and boat.

26 "Saint-Castin a Denonville, 2 Juillet 1687," in *Collection des Manuscrits contenant lettres, mémoires et autres documents historiques rélatifs a la Nouvelle-France*, 4 vols. (Quebec, 1883–85), 1: 400.

27 This really began with the French invasion of the Rhineland in 1688. For a good account see John B. Wolf, *Louis XIV* (New York, 1968), 446–90.

Quill pens, not even carbon paper, dominated the record keeping. Yet the personal authority of the monarch was needed before any major initiative could be undertaken. Even more than in the 1990s, government action and its impact was as much a matter of coincidence and happenstance as intent.

Nevertheless, there was a clear intent behind the appointment of Louis Alexandre des Friches de Menneval[28] as governor and commander of Acadia in 1687. He was not a member of a great noble family, but was of "good birth." He had been a career officer in the army and had earned the good opinion of Turenne. Now his task was to shore-up a neglected outpost of empire and re-establish French prestige in an area where it was felt to have deteriorated badly. He received detailed instructions about his task in April of 1687.[29]

Commentators have most often highlighted those sections of his instructions that required Menneval to prevent the English from trading and fishing in Acadia,[30] and certainly a great deal of space is devoted to these matters. Further, Menneval was given men, supplies, and the support of a light frigate, *La Friponne*, to carry out these instructions. There is no doubt that these actions had a major impact upon the colony.

Yet equally – if not more – interesting are the information and instructions contained in the second and third paragraphs of this document. Here the issue of the internal structure of Acadia is addressed and the King complains of those who "prétendent avoir les concessions exclusives sur vastes estendues dudit pais, meme avec la faculte d'accorder des concessions a d'autres" that such persons had become almost absentee landlords, occupying themselves "uniquement ... a la traite dans les bois, et dans une debauche scandaleuse," and were even going so far as to exercise "aussy des violences contres les Francois sous pretextes desdites concessions." Menneval was ordered to reimpose the authority of the Crown and given the right to despatch to France – "repasser en France" – any who refused to reform their ways and accept the new dispensations. Early Acadians using violence against the French? Arguing about the legality of the power of the Crown? Living lives of scandalous

28 See his biography by René Beaudry in *DCB*, 2: 182–4.
29 These are printed in *Collection des manuscrits*, 1: 396–9.
30 Rawlyk, *Nova Scotia's Massachusetts*, 53; and René Beaudry, *DCB*, 2: 182.

debauchery? In these phrases lies evidence about the reality of Acadian society at this time as opposed to what France might envisage.

The Acadian population at this time was small, but we have a fair amount of information about it. Three censuses have survived from the 1680s,[31] which is a large number even for a continent that liked to number its new inhabitants.[32] These censuses record, if somewhat erratically, information about sex distribution, family size, age distribution, the placing of settlements and the number of stock, as well as some idea of the amount of land cleared, and allow one to

31 The first is that submitted by Perrot and assembled by Jacques de Meulles. It has been printed twice in full nominal form, the latest being in *Bulletin des Recherches Historiques* (1932). The second was by a man named Gargas, compiled in 1687–8, printed in W. T. Morse, ed., *Acadiensis Nova* (London, 1935), 1: 144–5. The third census was taken in 1689: it is in AC, G1–466, 58–9 and has been published, with some inaccuracies, in Rameau de St Père, *Une Colonie Féodale en Amerique: L'Acadie, 1604–1881*, 2 vols. (Paris, 1881), 2: 403. A summary of these is in Clark, *Acadia*, 124. In assessing the information from these censuses, one has to be aware that they will not include all inhabitants, not even all the inhabitants of European descent. Few of those who compiled them have the honesty of the first census-taker of Acadie. This was a certain Father Molin who concluded his work by noting those who would not co-operate, among them Pierre Melanson, the tailor who sent his wife out to say that he would not reveal his age, or the number of cattle he had, or the amount of land under cultivation and furthermore that the priest must be mad to run about the streets asking such questions. Nevertheless, all of the enumerators would have encountered the unco-operative. Further, the work was undertaken among people for whom neither numeracy nor the division of time by accurate measurement of age was of particular importance. Finally, of course, each of those who compiled these statistics was his own secretary, recording data with a quill pen, and with no more aide-memoires than his own memory. Thus, the level of accuracy of the reports is limited. The limits, however, are those of omission rather than invention.

32 James Cassidy has noted that Americans seem always to have had a high propensity to count and that there were more than 124 counts of population for 29 American colonies between 1623 and 1775, all in response to demands for information from the British government. Jim Potter, "Demographic Development and Family Structure," in Greene and Pole, eds., *Colonial British America*, 134–5.

comment on a number of aspects of Acadian society in the late seventeenth century.[33]

First, the people were fertile and the children lived. Throughout the settlements the average family size seems to have been five or six children. In a study which extends beyond the three years of the census, and uses as well the few available parish records, Gysa Hynes found that the average number of children per family was seven, with many a family of ten, and a few of fourteen or more.[34] In common with the experience of much of New England, infant mortality was low. At least 75 percent of the children survived to adulthood. This was very different from Europe and from the Amerindian population. Similarly, those who survived the "seasoning period" had prospects of a considerably longer life than most of their contemporaries in the other collectives of humanity.

Second, the colony boasted only one significant area of settlement – Port Royal – where some two-thirds of those recorded resided. In Perrot's census in 1686 the number given is 583 people, made up of ninety-six families, with 218 boys and 177 girls under sixteen.[35] There are three other clusters of people, none of them anywhere rivalling Port Royal: Chedabucto, 20 people sorted into five families; Minas, 57 people gathered into ten families; and Beaubassin, 127 people making up seventeen families.[36] There were also a few scattered settlers reported at La Have (Mirligueche) and at Cap Sable; to the north of Beaubassin around the Miramichi; and at the mouth of the St John river, and elsewhere along the present-day New Brunswick–Maine coast.

Within three years, Minas became an attractive alternative to the leading settlement, Port Royal. In 1689 the total population for Port Royal was estimated at 461, whereas Minas totalled 164, only just over a third the size of Port Royal but more than three times its own

33 The publication of Stephen White's genealogical work on the period before 1713, now being concluded at the Centre d'études acadiennes, should enable scholars to give a much more detailed demographical analysis.

34 Gysa Hynes, "Some Aspects of the Demography of Port Royal, 1650–1755," in P.A. Buckner and David Frank, eds., *Atlantic Canada Before Confederation: The Acadiensis Reader*, 2 vols. 1 (Fredericton, 1985), 1: 11–25. This is a reprint of article in *Acadiensis* (autumn, 1973): 3–17.

35 This is an estimate since the census taker records these totals, but in the text does not record separately, either the names or ages of the girls. The boys, however, are named and their ages given.

36 AC, G1–466, 14–57.

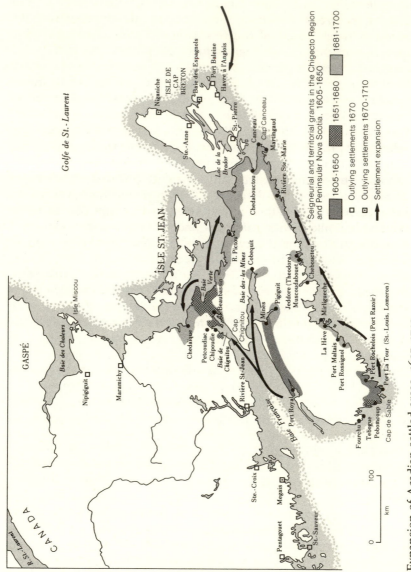

Expansion of Acadian settled areas, 1605–1710

Golfe de St.-Laurent

CANADA

R. St.-Laurent

GASPÉ

Baie des Chaleurs

Isle Miscou

Nipisiguit

Maramichy

ÎSLE ST. JEAN

ISLE DE CAP BRETON

Niganiche

Ste.-Anne

Baie des Espagnols

Port Baleine

St.-Pierre

Havre à l'Anglois

Lac de la Brador

Pentagouet

St.-Sauveur

Megais

Ste.-Croix

Port Royal

Baie Française

Rivière St.-Jean

Chédaïque

Petcoudiac

Chipoudie

Baie de Chignitou

Cap Chignitou

Baie Verte

Beaubassin

Baie des-les Mines

R. Pictou

Cobequit

Mines

Pigiguit

Jeddore (Theodore)

Muscoudabouet

Chebouctou

Chédabouctou

Rivière Ste.-Marie

Martingaud

Cap Canceau

Canceau

Mirliguèche

La Hève

Port Maltais

Port Rossignol

Port Rochelois (Port Razoir)

Port La Tour (St.-Louis, Lomeron)

Fourchu

Tebogue

Pobomcoup

Cap de Sable

0   100

km

Seigneurial and territorial grants in the Chigecto Region
and Peninsular Nova Scotia, 1605–1650

1605-1650   1651-1680   1681-1700

☐ Outlying settlements 1670

⊡ Outlying settlements 1670-1710

→ Settlement expansion

size of three years before. It has generally been accepted that migration to the Minas area was mostly the movement of young people, an interpretation supported by a comment of Gargas, who had been despatched to Port Royal in 1687 to act as secretary to the colony. Gargas deplored the fact that the Governor "allows the young sons of the colonists to go and settle elsewhere along the coast, where they do nothing but hunt or negotiate with the natives."[37] However, closer examination shows that Acadian experience was no different from that of their English neighbours. Recent studies of early New Englanders and Virginians have shown that there was considerable mobility among settlers of all ages after their arrival in America.[38] It is clear that the lead in establishing the new settlements within Acadia was taken by families who had already spent considerable time at Port Royal. Pierre Melanson, who had refused to co-operate with the first census-taker in 1671, was the prime mover behind the Minas Basin settlement.[39] By 1686 he had mellowed somewhat in his attitude to inquiry, and it is reported that he was fifty-four years old and had nine children, ranging in age from twenty years old to a new-born.[40] The moving spirits behind Beaubassin were Jacques Bourgeois and his wife. Although well-established in Port Royal in 1671, with a family of ten children, thirty-three cattle, a small flock of sheep and five arpents of cleared land, they too sought a new frontier.

There has been little written in the twentieth century about Acadian society that compares its development with either that of the valley of the St Lawrence or with the formation of northern New England.[41] In part, this is undoubtedly because Acadia is perceived

37 "Sojourn of Gargas in Acadie, 1687–1688," in Morse, *Acadiensis Nova*, 178.

38 Potter, "Demographic Development," in Greene and Pole, eds., *Colonial British America*, 134.

39 On this see the excellent, if brief, study by Brenda Dunn, *Les Acadiens des Mines* (Ottawa, 1985).

40 "Jacques de Meulles' Census," partially printed in Beamish Murdoch, *A History of Nova Scotia or Acadie*, 3 vols. (Halifax, 1865), 1: 170.

41 Rameau de St Père, *Une colonie féodale en Amerique*, (Paris, 1881), was a conscious attempt to consider what feudalism and the seigneurial system meant for Acadie. It is handicapped to a very large extent by St Père's misunderstanding of feudalism. His research in primary documents relating to Acadie, however, is of a very high quality. In his pivotal study, *The Seigneurial System in Early Canada: A Geographical Study* (Madison, 1968), Cole Harris concentrated on the valley of the St Lawrence.

as insignificant, but it is also due to the confused nature of the land-ownership question in Acadia. In my view, if control of the colony by England between 1654 and 1670 did nothing else, it made non-sense of any seigneurial structure as the basis for land-ownership within the colony.[42] The history of Acadia in these years has never been fully told. Fifteen years is a long period of time in the development of a colonial society. English control brought, not only the disruption of one series of ideas about how the colony should function but also the introduction of alternative views. Crowne and Temple, who administered the colony during these years, did so via Boston and with the English ideas of yeoman and tenant as the background to their policies.[43] Even after the return of the colony to French control, too much had happened for the seigneuries that were granted to be more than simple land titles, without any real possibility of sub-infeudation.[44] This was recognized, to a certain extent, even by those who wished a seigneurial system to prevail. After 1670, when new concessions were made to proprietors in Acadia, acknowledgment was often made of the rights of settlers who had already established themselves, without legally registered title. For example, grants made in 1676 to Leneuf de la Vallière of land in Beaubassin contained specific clauses exempting the colonists previously established there from the imposition of new obligations.[45]

There is no doubt, too, that the tangled history of the rivalries between the earlier explorers and the traders of Acadie – La Tour, d'Aulnay, Denys, Le Borgne[46] – had helped to undermine the establishment of a seigneurial system. Documents about the attempt

---

42 There are adequate records for this period. See in particular British Museum Additional Mss. 11411; Public Record Office Series M–371, and M–381; and PANS, Series A–1 and A–2.

43 Howard Russell, abridged by Mark Lapping, *A Long Deep Furrow: Three Centuries of Farming in New England* (Hanover, NH, 1982); and John Weller, *History of the Farmstead* (London, 1982).

44 On the whole issue of attitudes towards territoriality by Europeans in North America, see Robert David Sack, *Human Territoriality: Its Theory and History* (Cambridge, 1986), 127–68. On the issue of seigneuries in Acadie see Clark, *Acadia*, 113–21.

45 de St Père, *Une colonie féodale*, Table 1, 168.

46 Some flavour of these disputes is given in Elizabeth Jones, *Gentlemen and Jesuits: Quests for Glory and Adventure in the Early Days of New France* (Toronto, 1986).

made by Sieur de Fontenu in 1699 to disentangle who had what title
to what land in Acadie, and on what conditions, reveal – above all
– confusion.[47] For present purposes, what is important is that Acadians were relatively unfettered by ideas of a rank-ordered system
of land-ownership. Of course, when the colony was controlled by
France, the official theory of land ownership in Acadia was that land
was to be granted by the Crown to a seigneur, who would in turn
grant land to tenants on specific terms, requiring services on both
sides. The seigneur would be required to provide such communal
facilities as grist mills, ovens, and the organization of other settlers.
The tenant would pay some form of rent, in labour, kind, coin, or
a combination of all three. In practice, however, Acadians were much
more free-ranging in settlement than a strict seigneurial system
would have permitted. It is true that even in Quebec the seigniorial
system was by no means uniformly imposed. There is no doubt,
however, that the St Lawrence valley displayed many features of
such a system, from the communal requirements of road building
to the manner of surveying and parcelling-out land.[48] The impact
of English control, together with the Acadians' knowledge of the
practices of Maine and Massachusetts, led to the creation of a settlement pattern that had almost nothing in common with a seigneurial system. Acadians were much more a collectivity of yeoman
and tenant farmers, fishermen and craftsmen, than a community of
habitants.

Indeed, there is far more in common than is often recognized in
the colonial developments of northern New England and of Acadia.
The parallel is particularly noticeable in the spatial order of the communities. In contrast to much of France and England, the Acadian
landscape, in James Lemon's words, "carried the marks of the dispersed society, one that was organized extensively more than in-
tensively."[49] The nuclear village, constructed around a green and
church and surrounded by open fields and common lands, so often
found in England and quite common in western France at this time,
was not the seventeenth-century North American norm. Instead, to

47 Many of these have been printed in Placide Gaudet, "Les seigneuries
de l'ancienne Acadie," *Bulletin des Recherches Historiques* 33 (1927): 343–
7.

48 It would be invidious to select only a page or so of Harris' work on
Quebec, but see in particular, *The Seigneurial System*, 106–7.

49 James Lemon, "Spatial Order: Households in Local Communities and
Regions," in Greene and Pole, eds., *Colonial British America*, 86.

quote Lemon again, "the predominant pattern was one of individual farmsteads, often initially much dispersed but gradually coalescing into apparently loose rural communities and neighbourhoods. In most places these individual farmsteads were separated one from another by contiguous fields."[50] This description can be applied not only to Beaubassin and Minas, but to Port Royal as well. Perrot, in 1686, had complained bitterly of the way in which the people of that community scattered themselves "tres esloigne les un les autres," and as far as he was concerned, their main purpose was to evade even the minimal constraints imposed by the official life in the centre of the settlement and to "s'entretenir plus facilement dans la debauche avec les sauvaggesses."[51]

This last comment brings into focus a point too often neglected: Acadia was a peopled land when the Europeans arrived and those who then lived in it, Micmac and Malecite, were an obvious and crucial part of life in the new settlements. Recent scholarly debate about Euro-American contacts has recognized that the terms previously used to relate the history of the meeting of peoples from two continents are not only inadequate but often misleading. To talk about the discovery of America without acknowledging that there was an equivalent discovery of Europe for those who lived there has become recognizably inept.[52] It is now acknowledged that the people indigenous to the Americas had their own complex history, their own religions that were mystical and sophisticated, and their own cultural lives of intricate subtlety before Europeans ever reached their shores.[53] This recognition of the independent reality

50 Ibid., 90.
51 "'Relation de l'Acadie,' Perrot, 9th August, 1686," AC, C-11, D2, 1.
52 The publication of *The Great Frontier* by Walter Prescott Webb in 1952 has often been taken as the crucial academic demonstration of the fact that the Americas were not invented by Europeans. Ever since then, the scholarly community has made valiant efforts, sometimes successful, sometimes not, to temper Eurocentric interpretations of the migration of Europeans across the Atlantic.
53 It is not simply that the work of ethnohistorians such as James Axtell and Bruce Trigger has presented the past in such a way as to demonstrate the humanity of the Amerindian peoples. There have also been meticulous studies such as D. Crosby, *The Columbia Exchange: Biological and Cultural Consequences of 1492* (Greenwich, Ct., 1972). A work which presents a synthesis of much of this thinking is D.W. Meinig, *The Shaping of America: A Geographical Perspective on 500 Years of History: Atlantic America, 1492–1800* (New Haven, 1986).

of Micmac and Malecite life, however, does not make the task of understanding the relationship of "native and newcomer," to use Bruce Trigger's phrase, any easier.

Ever since the publication in 1937 of A.G. Bailey's pioneering work, *The Conflict of European and Eastern Algonkian Cultures, 1504–1700*, there has been little excuse for treating the Micmac peoples as a relatively unimportant aspect of the Acadian environment. This work stressed the importance of Micmac friendliness to the early settlers of Acadie.[54] But the prejudiced attitude of the seventeenth-century French officials about the Micmac undoubtedly coloured later accounts. In the light of unfavourable reports by French officials, such as that written by Perrot in 1686, the essentially co-operative relationship between the colonists and Micmacs has been overlooked. Much less is known about it than one would like, and Clark's comment, made in 1968, that "the absorption of Micmac by the Acadian community has not been well studied," remains true today, more than twenty years later.[55]

We know even less about the Micmac absorption of the Acadian. The research that James Axtell reported in his article "The White Indians of Colonial America," on the ways in which a good many of European descent were assimilated by the Amerindian people, has yet to spark a comparable inquiry for Acadian and Micmac.[56] Yet Micmac recruitment from among the newcomers to compensate – from the Micmac point of view – for some part of the demographic holocaust that they had suffered, is certainly highly likely. There is no doubt that the mortality rate among the Micmac, if not as high as in the sixteenth, continued high enough during the seventeenth century to be of grave concern for the community.[57] Nor is there doubt that such affliction demanded an openness to any possible remedy. As Axtell has written, while the individual endured the personal "psychological despair of having to watch family and friends cut down,"[58] there was the added stress of contemporary

---

54 A.G. Bailey *The Conflict of European and Eastern Algonkian Cultures, 1504–1700*, 2^d ed, (Toronto, 1969). See in particular 8–21.

55 Clark, *Acadia*, 128.

56 "The White Indians of Colonial America" has been published in James Axtell, *The European and the Indian*, ch. 7.

57 Martin, *Keepers of the Game*, 43–51.

58 Axtell, "The English Impact on Indian Culture," in *The European and the Indian*, 250.

agony for the whole community. Such devastation brought the social disintegration of the Micmac very close.[59] As Axtell has written:

The loss of family members tore gaping holes in the extensive web of clans and kinship that shaped an Indian's identity as much as language and residence. Technological skills leadership, and the group's corporate memory were lost with key adult members, especially elders who, with infants, possessed the least resistance. Political succession [was in] ... disarray. Settlement patterns, broken. But perhaps most important, the natives' religious beliefs, cosmological assumptions and social morale were battered by the inexplicable fate that had befallen them, predisposing them to seek the material and spiritual help of the newcomers.[60]

In such circumstances healthy new recruits, especially those belonging to the new and powerful community, would be both sought and welcomed.

From the point of view of the European, the prospect of living among the Micmac had very definite attractions. They were, and are, a handsome people. Their society was one possessed of a considerable sense of commitment between its members, much open expression of affection among its people, and a life-style that emphasized mobility and a modicum of adventure. There are a number of questions about the general organization of Acadian family life that can be more readily answered if the relationship between Acadian and Micmac is treated as an ongoing contact between people who had the good sense to appreciate one another. The extraordinary stress upon the sexual morality of the Acadians would become more plausible if Acadian settlements formed part of a larger and more flexible human community. The cordial alliance that was built between the two peoples, Acadian and Micmac, over the next seventy years becomes more explicable if we accept that there were considerable family ties between the two groups. One needs to remember that comments about debauchery and licentiousness come from observers whose beliefs about the proper conduct of sexuality excluded any appreciation of non-Christian morality. Many European minds could not admit the possibility that personal commitment and a stable family life could develop between individuals without the ratification of the Church. The Micmac marriage rite, the public celebration in the community of matrimonial intent, was

59 Bailey, *The Conflict* is convinced that this did in fact occur.
60 Axtell, "The English Impact," in *The European and the Indian*.

not accepted as legitimate by most official European visitors to Acadie. Much more work on these issues needs to be undertaken. Suffice it to say at this point that the Micmac were certainly positive contributors to the survival and flourishing of the Acadians.

It is clear, too, quite apart from the question of kin, that even if further research should disprove the existence of close familial connections between the two societies, the Micmac had considerable economic and cultural influence on the Acadians in the late seventeenth century. The importance of the fur trade to Port Royal and the outer settlements has rarely been examined, and the place of the Micmac in this activity has yet to be estimated. Clark merely noted that the fur trade declined steadily after mid-century, "but continued to yield cargoes for France up until the English take-over."[61] Other forms of economic interaction warrant mention. A man called Gargas was a minor bureaucrat, a kind of government surveyor, who spent the winter of 1687–88 in Acadie. In his report for that year, one of his many complaints was the poor price paid by Robineau Villebon for the skins brought to him by the colonists.[62] Since this trade was one of the few sources through which specie would be acquired by the community, it is even more urgent to understand its ramifications. Further, as John Reid has emphasized in his writings, trade made the Acadians the very reverse of an isolated peasantry. Whether smuggling or keeping within the bounds of law, Acadians met and observed people from Louisbourg and Boston, not to mention the Caribbean.

Fishing and agriculture formed the basis of the Acadian economy. But there is a continuing debate over the standard of living provided the Acadians by these activities. At the time, officials from France complained bitterly about lackadaisical Acadian farming practices. Yet the details of the contemporary census offer evidence of an agriculture that provided a good standard of nutrition for the settlers.[63] When Bishop St Vallier made his pastoral visit in 1686, he was clearly of two minds as to the level of prosperity of Beaubassin. On the one hand, he noted that these settlers had captured the cattle left wandering on Sable Island by de Razilly, nearly fifty years earlier,

---

61 Clark, *Acadia*, 181.
62 "Sojourn of Gargas in Acadie, 1687–1688," in Morse, *Acadiensis Nova* 1: 176.
63 On this, and on the impact of nutrition on fertility, see Hynes, "Some Aspects of the Demography," in Buckner and Frank, *Atlantic Canada Before Confederation*.

and were in process of establishing considerable herds from this stock. He also mentioned that fishing was pursued with interest and that grain was available. On the other hand, he considered the clothing poor and noted that the community could barely produce enough cloth, through their own efforts, to clothe themselves adequately.[64]

Gargas, by contrast, deplored the general state of all the settlements and considered that there were scarcely three people of the entire population who could make a fishing net. As to Beaubassin itself, he considered it a place to be known by "its many fogs." Yet another commentator, Jacques de Meulles, the Intendant of New France, considered that Beaubassin flourished. According to him the inhabitants were reasonably lodged and each family was provided with a good-sized herd of cattle, as well as twenty or so pigs and the same number of sheep. He thought that the spinning and weaving done was quite adequate to clothe the families.[65] There was more agreement among these three on the state of Port Royal, allowing for the congenital bad-temper of Gargas and the general distemper of de Meulles. All thought Port Royal could become an impressive establishment, given intelligent administration and the expenditure of enough money.

The nub of the argument is really about quality of life and the difference between marginal economic existence and self-sufficient communities who support themselves without famine or dearth.[66] By the late 1680s, Acadia can best be summed up as a colony that had taken root. While life was hard, it was not a desperate, unremitting struggle for existence by a population unable to keep its children alive. The colonists by this time had begun to exploit a complex set of resources which allowed its population to be self-sustaining, able to provide themselves with the basic necessities of shelter, food, and clothing. There was commerce, and the continual official French complaints that such commerce was controlled by Boston merchants serves only to underline the fact that it did exist and was important.

64 "Voyages de St. Vallier" in H. Têtu and C.O. Gagnon, eds., *Mandements, lettres pastorales et circulaires des évèques de Quebec* 2 vols. (1887), 1: 217.

65 "Account of the Voyage of de Meulles to Acadie Oct. 11, 1685–July 6, 1986," in Morse, *Acadiensis Nova*, 1: 103, ff.

66 Discussion of the difference between "subsistence farming" and "self-sufficient farming" is to be found in Russell, *A Long, Deep Furrow*, 58, ff. See also Peter Benes, ed., *The Farm* (Boston, 1988).

Although trade was not strictly necessary for the survival of the
Acadians, it supplied the metal goods, guns, and ammunition vital
in Acadian life.

Little has yet been written about the structure of Acadian society
at the close of the 1680s. The economy demanded considerable and
almost continuous labour. The various clusters of settlers provided
for their own needs by combining agriculture, hunting, fishing, gar-
dening, and trade in many different fashions. In so doing, they
developed a society that had considerable internal mobility among
the individuals, but nevertheless knew gradations of economic resource. While there was little outright destitution and even less
considerable wealth, there were considerable differences reported
by the various observers in the numbers of cattle each family owned,
the amount of land cleared, and flocks pastured. The complex kin
structures mitigated economic divisions, but Acadian society should
not be envisaged as one without internal hierarchies. Certainly the
definition of peasant used by Allan Greer in his seminal work on
Quebec cannot be applied, without considerable modification, to a
people whose daily lives combined farming, fishing, and hunting
in such a complex manner.[67] For Greer, a peasant is someone whose
life is based on "small scale agriculture," the technology of which is
very simple and the labour force made up of the family. Economically, such people are self-sufficient but rarely have completely free
ownership of their land. A proportion of their produce, moreover,
is appropriated by a more privileged class.[68] It is true that agriculture
was an essential ingredient of Acadian life. However, it was not the
only such ingredient and, above all, it was a pursuit that in the
Minas and Beaubassin settlements demanded a community, rather
than a familial labour force.

As the title to this chapter has suggested, the 1680s saw a settlement established in Acadia, not a distinctive community identity
forged. But by then the colony had, in establishing its settlements,
at least provided a foundation which would allow the later development of a unique community. By the conclusion of the 1680s,
Acadia already was demographically self-generating, although after
1686 there would be the addition of a greater number of migrants
to the society than has hitherto been believed. The construction of
a distinctive identity lay in the future. What is present at this date

67 Allan Greer, *Peasant, Lord, and Merchant: Rural Society in Three Parishes,
1740–1840* (Toronto, 1985).
68 Ibid., xi.

is a number of different attributes which would finally combine to mould such an identity.

Various questions about the settlement at this time remain to be answered. First, there is the whole question of the Acadian family and household matters, about which, paradoxically, we seem to know far too much and not nearly enough. Intense genealogical interest has resulted in an appreciation of individual family descent, but more general questions concerning relationships within the family and the connection between family and household remain unanswered. While it is generally accepted that pre-deportation Acadia was a society for which Marxist analysis is not particularly useful, the work on property holdings still has to be done, so that we know whether the Leblancs or the Melansons or the Gaudets had any particular status in relation to one another. We are not clear as to the physical environment for the family: what is an Acadian household? What is the intersection between individual life and family cycle? All one can say is that the Acadian settlements in 1686 were built from the family units and that there seems to have been no major imbalance in sexual ratio at any particular time.

Then there is the question of the heritage of the Acadian migrants. Where did they actually come from? When? And how? We have a considerable amount of information to answer these questions, and the work of Geneviève Massignon continues to prove invaluable.[69] But very little expansion of this work has taken place, and the true heritage of diversity brought from Europe is frequently underestimated. The extraordinary multiplicity of custom and language in seventeenth-century France has not been given its due. France, then and now, is in European terms a large country – at least twice as big as the United Kingdom. In the seventeenth century the population was relatively large: some 17 to 20 million as opposed to the roughly 5 million who lived in the British Isles. Most importantly, in the seventeenth century France was a much more fragmented society than her rival, one which its rulers from Henry IV to Louis XIV, and from Sully to Mazarin, continuously struggled to unify. From the cream, butter, and cider country of Normandy to the garlic, red wine, and olive country of Marseilles, from the dry chalk of Champagne to the slope of the Pyrenees, the country was a complex kaleidoscope of customs, of traditions, and of dialects so different as to be, for practical purposes, distinct languages. All the various sectors of France had different relations with the power of

69 Geneviève Massignon, *Les Parlers Français d'Acadie*, (Paris, 1962).

the Crown and the central governmental structures of the state. From the terms of contract to which Brittany had finally agreed, when joining France in 1491, to the ancient customs of the Ile-de-France, innumerable variations of authority were recognized within the country. In Champagne the provincial estates met tri-annually, dominated by the land-owning class. In the Gironde, they almost never met but were dominated by the peasantry when they did. Voltaire remarked that one changed laws in France as often as one changed horses. Thus, the Leblancs, coming from Poitou, would have different assumptions about the ways in which authority was exercised than the Roys arriving from St Malo with the customs of Brittany as their norm. The Bastarache from the Basque country would have very different ideas about the rights of property holders than the Arsenaults from Rochfort, that marshy city which, as late as the eighteenth century, was referred to as a place of fevers and barbarity.[70]

The archaeological work of Alaric and Gretchen at Pentagoet in present-day Maine has amply demonstrated that the migrants brought with them a considerable amount of everyday material culture from their former lives, as well as European cosmological beliefs.[71] The use of tools such as axes and guns, ploughs and spades, was only part of what was transferred. Patterns of clothes, techniques of cooking, ways of working wood and of spinning nets, and the new art of knitting (something that was only just becoming commonplace in seventeenth-century England and France) – all would be part of the migrants' repertoire of skills from Europe, in varying degrees and in varying ways. The publication of the archaeological work now being done on the Belle-Isle site in south-western Nova Scotia will soon enrich our knowledge in this area.

This plurality of political expectation from diverse regions of France and considerable breadth of material culture was equalled by the diversity of social traditions the migrants brought. For example, the expectations for women differed widely. In Brittany, women were expected to be able to mend fishing nets and to help with the oyster beds. In Béarn and the districts bordering on the Basque lands,

70 Eugene Weber, *Peasants into Frenchmen: The Modernization of Rural France, 1870–1914* (Stanford, 1976), 4.

71 *The French at Pentagoet 1635–1674: An Archaeological Portrait of the Acadian Frontier*, Occasional Publications in Maine Archaeology/Special Publications of the New Brunswick Museum (Saint John, 1987), in particular 267, ff.

women were expected to be able to tend the gardens and run the households while the men drove the herds and flocks to Bordeaux. The legal position and rights of inheritance of wives and daughters also altered from district to district. As important as any secular conventions were the expectations of the religious authorities, and these would be very different according to whether the accepted interpretation of Christianity in the area was Catholic or Huguenot, and whether it was strongly enforced.[72] The diverse heritage of migrants from France to North America has to be kept fully in mind as one imagines the beginnings of the Francophone experience here. What needs to be looked at is how, in Acadia, the family structures and kin networks melded the various individual inheritances together. As has been suggested, the recruitment of settlers for Acadia was a haphazard process and there was no continuous, overarching civic authority forcing conformity to predefined political and social norms. The polity which emerges as Acadian is something that was evolved by people from the Loire, Scotland, Poitou, and the Micmac communities. Much remains to be discovered about the way in which individuals of particular heritage gained the support of their peers to become leaders of the Acadians.

It is important to turn at this point from the description of group-linked characteristics of the developing colony to the matter of the individual. In the development of the distinctive identity of any group, it is the vision of the individual that drives the people. The web of community, family, economic structures, and political institutions are important, above all, because of their connection with the individual. It is the single human being that is the building block; it is the single human being that can be characterised for theoretical purposes by one or more of his/her component qualities and attributes; and it is the individual human action and reaction to the surrounding world that brings changes to this world. While the scholarship about collectivities is a crucial tool for understanding past societies, such scholarship obviously centers on only part of human experience. It needs the balance of the single biography, something which brings the reality of personal variation to the study of past process. While their biographies may be relatively unknown, Acadia had among its inhabitants various movers and shakers, individuals whose social behaviour was one of considerable enterprise

72 The work by A. Armegaud, *La famille et l'enfant en France et en Angle-terre du xvi au xviii siecle–aspects demographiques* (Paris, 1975) is the most erudite short guide through these thickets.

and independence. As early as the 1680s, one can find considerable records of disputes over rights among the settlers.[73] The image of a united, contented peasantry is shattered, to be replaced by the normal picture of rural politics: people concerned with property and prestige. There are also similar records of the beginning of another Acadian characteristic: that of arguing with constituted authority. Gargas has recorded his own arguments over a canoe with Bourg, whom he characterized as "one of the most rebellious and independent inhabitants of Acadie ... [possessing] more relations than almost anyone else in Port Royal."[74]

The intellectual history of the Acadians of the 1680s and the elements of their cultural universe at that time have been, as yet, barely considered. The permanent presence of the institutions of both civil and religious authority had really only just been established. The relationship of Church to State authority in the colony was unclear and the recent Revocation of the Edict of Nantes was only just beginning to make an impact. de Meulles commented, in 1686, that a number of the ships at Canso were crewed by recently converted Huguenots and he noted that he "stayed (here) three days to give several ordinances and to remedy the abuses which had crept in among these new converts."[75] The settlements certainly welcomed the visit of St Vallier, Bishop of Quebec. They constructed wooden churches. But the place of Catholicism in Acadian lives was still not settled and our picture of it owes far too much to the wishful thinking of devout nineteenth-century Acadian leaders. Knowledge about the reality of Acadian political life at this time is equally hazy. There is as yet no clear account of how effective the officials dispatched from France were in Acadia, nor of how far the legal structures of the Acadians reflected any practices common in France.

Similarly, knowledge of the development of artistic abilities among the settlers is in its infancy. One can only point out that the migrants had brought with them their heritage of folk-tale and music.[76] As

---

73 de Meulles comments on the way in which he settled disputes and drew up necessary ordinances so that the settlers might live in peace. Morse, *Acadiensis Nova*, 1: 104, ff.

74 "Sojourn of Gargas in Acadie, 1687–8," in Morse, *Acadiensis Nova*, 1: 168–9.

75 Ibid., "Voyage of monsieur de Meulles to Acadie," 1: 117.

76 This is ably documented by Antonine Maillet, *Rabelais et les traditions populaires en Acadie* (Laval, 1971) and Catherine Jolicoeur, *Les plus belles legends acadiennes* (Stanke, 1981).

to the material culture, while it is clear that the Acadians were adapting some of the technology they had imported from Europe to the particular needs of the new environment and also adopting Micmac fishing weirs and canoes among other useful artifacts, once more knowledge about the evolution of a distinctive Acadian style is in its infancy. Questions about the Acadians' homes: the sizes and types of houses (an area of study in which Jean-Claude Dupont has been a marvellous pioneer),[77] their furnishings, and their relation to outbuildings are now being illuminated by archaeological work, such as that being pursued on the upper Belle-Isle marsh in Annapolis County, Nova Scotia. A detailed synthesis of what has recently become known about material culture is much needed.

But, all in all, Acadia existed in 1690 as a community in the sum of its parts distinct from any other European settlement in North America. This distinctiveness was even more pronounced two generations later, when an Acadian identity was fully established.

77 Jean-Claude Dupont, *Heritage d'Acadie* (Lemeac, 1977).

CHAPTER TWO

The 1730s: Identity Established

At the close of the seventeenth century there was a colony known as "Acadia or Nova Scotia." A generation later, there was an Acadian people. The development of a recognizable, new, separate identity by a community depends as much on demographic and economic variables as on the development of a particular combination of social, cultural, and political variables that is unique to the emerging group. There has to be a critical mass of people who believe in their own distinctiveness as a group. Specific ways of organizing community life, providing food and shelter, and forming the ideas of the next generation will not lead to a unique community identity unless enough people see themselves precisely as members of that distinctive new community. By the end of the seventeenth century one can distinguish in Acadia many of the social customs, religious beliefs, political norms, economic practices, and artistic traditions that would blend in a unique fashion to form the distinctive Acadian identity. However, it is not until the 1730s – a generation later – that an Acadian people can be said to exist.

In 1700 the colony was both demographically self-generating and economically self-sustaining. While newcomers were still arriving in the colony, population increase was largely due to the natural increase of those already settled. The fertility rate was comparable to the highest rates then found in France.[1] Trade was needed by the colony for all kinds of tools and weaponry. But the interruption of supplies from Europe or Boston to Port Royal no longer meant the immediate destitution of the tiny villages of the Minas Basin and

1 Gysa Hynes, "Some Aspects of the Demography of Port Royal, 1650–1755," *Acadiensis* 3 (1973): 14 fn. 48.

the growing establishments of Beaubassin. Scarcities so produced were not great enough to impinge drastically on fertility. The crucial differences between Acadia in 1700 and Acadia in 1730 lay in the nature of Acadian politics, in the rapidity of demographic growth, and in the development of social and cultural complexities.

For the Acadians, two of the most politically important events of these years were the fall of Port Royal in 1710, to an expedition out of New England, and the subsequent confirmation of that victory, three years later, in the provisions of the Treaty of Utrecht in 1713.[2] This agreement ended the series of haphazard conflicts and outright wars that had been fought between England and France since 1689. Unlike the Treaty of Ryswick of 1697, which effected only a brief respite, the Treaty of Utrecht brought peace for a generation.[3] It was a Treaty by which France retained a considerable amount of her power in Europe at the price of lessening authority in North America.[4] By its terms, France kept control of the St Lawrence, Cape Breton Island, and what we know as Prince Edward Island, as well as other islands in the Gulf of St Lawrence. France did relinquish to Great Britain all claims to Newfoundland, except some fishing rights, and to Hudson's Bay. The Treaty also stipulated that "All Nova Scotia or Acadia, comprehended within its ancient boundaries; as also the city of Port Royal now called Annapolis Royal, and all other things in these parts which depend on the said lands and islands, together with the dominion, property and possession of the said islands, lands and places, and all rights whatever by treaties, or any other way attained, which the most christian king, the crown of France, or any the subjects thereof, have hitherto had to the said islands, lands and places, and to the inhabitants of the same, are

2 George Rawlyk, *Nova Scotia's Massachusetts: A study of Massachusetts–Nova Scotia Relations, 1630 to 1784* (Montreal, 1978), 116–23.

3 For a good brief account of the international story in these years see I.K. Steele, *Guerillas and Grenadiers: The Struggle for Canada* (Toronto, 1969). For more detail concerning Acadian-Nova Scotian matters see Rawlyk, *Nova Scotia's Massachusetts*.

4 Utrecht, circular: "Lords of Trade to Nicholson, with Proclamation of Peace and copy of the Treaty of Utrecht, May 8th, Whitehall, 1713." The clauses relating to Canada are printed in number of places, including Gustave Lanctot, *A History of Canada*, 3 vols., vol. 3, *From the Treaty of Utrecht to the Treaty of Paris, 1713–1763* (Toronto, 1965), 215–17; and B. Murdoch, *A History of Nova Scotia or Acadia*, 3 vols., (Halifax, 1865), 1: 332.

yielded and made over to the queen of Great Britain, and to her crown for ever." The Acadians had certain rights embodied in other clauses in the Treaty. They were granted the liberty "to remove themselves within a year to any other place, as they shall think fit, together with all their moveable effects." If any decided to remain, they were "to be subject to the Kingdom of Great Britain" and "to enjoy the free exercise of their religion, according to the usage of the Church of Rome, as far as the laws of Great Britain allow the same." The latter provisions were further amplified in a royal letter to Francis Nicholson, sent on 23 June 1713.[5] Nicholson had been appointed governor of the colony the previous year. In his commission he was bidden to grant to those Acadians who are willing to "Continue our Subjects to retain and Enjoy their said lands and Tenements without any Lett or Molestation as fully and freely as other our Subjects do, or may possess their lands and Estates, or to sell the same if they shall rather chose to remove elsewhere."[6]

A great many elements in these provisions would complicate the lives of all parties in the years to come, partly because the treaty was, inevitably, Eurocentric. As K.G. Davies has written, "England's gains at the Treaty of Utrecht are sometimes advanced to prove the emergence of America as a major concern of European diplomacy by 1713; they could just as well, perhaps better, be used to prove the opposite."[7] Its North American provisions were shaped with some acknowledgment of the needs of New England and New France, but the priorities of the diplomats lay elsewhere. What seemed to many contemporary European diplomats like fairly minor alterations in the agreed restructuring of Anglo-French spheres of influence in North America, would later prove to have been changes decisive for establishing the balance of power on that continent.

The example of "Acadia or Nova Scotia" is very much a case in point. From the viewpoint of Europe, the major difference that Utrecht brought for "Acadia or Nova Scotia" was a change in its status from a not overly inhabited territory recognized as French, with disputed boundaries, into a similarly under-populated territory recognized as English, with disputed boundaries. Yet from the Acadian viewpoint, the change would be crucial. By this diplomatic decision, their circumstances were altered from those of a people

5 This letter is printed in full in Murdoch, *History of Nova Scotia*, 333.

6 Commission, October 20th, NA, NSE, 7, no. 3.

7 K.G. Davies, *The North Atlantic World in the Seventeenth Century* (Minneapolis, 1974), 308.

on the periphery of French power to those of a border people of the English empire. International agreement had made them the legitimate subjects of the British Crown, should they remain on the lands they had settled. It had also ensured the continued presence in their immediate neighbourhood of their former political masters.

French power, after all, had only been reduced, not eradicated. France and settlers of French descent remained a major force in North America. France "still enjoyed ... the control and possession of the two great rivers of North America [the St Lawrence and the Mississippi] which in each case gave an entrance to the very heart of that continent."[8] In the view of one French-Canadian historian, Gustave Lanctot, Canada "emerged from the war with her essential territory from the Gulf [of St Lawrence] to the Great Lakes intact, with a reformed economy and an optimistic and confident spirit."[9] As far as the Acadians were concerned, it meant a continuing French presence in their universe. French power was legitimately ensconced close to their major settlements and French policy very quickly reasserted its authority with the development of Ile Royale (Cape Breton), including the foundation of Louisbourg in 1720.

At the same time, there was no doubt that the English were now the governors of the colony, trying both to make Nova Scotia a useful imperial outpost and to make the Acadians live within the terms of the treaty. At the outset the English were unsure as to whether the Acadians were a temporarily conquered people or prospective British subjects, partly because most Europeans fully expected the Acadians to move to French territory.[10] They did not. The Acadians considered themselves the rightful inhabitants of the lands on which they lived, not just negotiable assets to be moved about as pawns for the purposes of a distant empire. Many of the adults of the community (those who had been more than five years old in 1690) had previous

8 L.H. Gipson, *The British Empire Before The American Revolution*. 14 vols. Vol. 5, *Zones of International Friction: The Great Lakes Frontier, Canada, The West Indies, India, 1748–1754* (New York, 1942), 80.
9 Lanctot, *A History of Canada*, 2: 228.
10 This is a point of some importance. A short discussion of it is found in N.E.S. Griffiths: "The Acadians," *DCB*, 4: xvii-xxxi. Lengthier discussions of the issue are given by J.B. Brebner, *New England's Outpost* (New York, 1927), 65–9; and Antoine Blanchard, *Le Drame Acadien depuis 1604* (Montreal, 1936), 250 ff. See also Bernard Pottier, "Acadian Settlement on Ile Royale 1713–1734," MA thesis, Ottawa University, 1967.

experience of the English as the source of authority within the colony. It was with no great psychological effort, therefore, that the Acadians set about working out the conditions for their existence under the new dispensation. Britain faced the problem of governing her latest colony which, she quickly discovered, had a continually expanding population and whose Acadian elders were bent upon having considerable say in the way in which power would be exercised over their community.

In assessing British policy towards the Acadians, it helps to be clear about what sort of a power Great Britain was at the opening of the eighteenth century. Two issues in particular are crucial here: the contemporary attitude towards Roman Catholicism in Britain, and the priority given the development of colonial policy by the British government.[11] There is neither time nor space to present this complex society fully here, but a number of points should be made. In 1713, the year of Utrecht, Great Britain had, in some senses, been an imperial power for about two hundred years. While considerably more centralized than France in the seventeenth and eighteenth centuries, the lands controlled by the monarchs of England were by no means the unified state of today. However clearly their writ ran through Wales (the act of Union between the two countries having been passed in 1536), its people spoke a different language, many of its social customs were different from those of England, and its main religious beliefs were beginning to diverge considerably from those of England. Within a generation, Methodism would find its most dedicated congregations among the mining valleys and high hills of this land. Similarly, while Scotland had accepted the Act of Union in 1707, there is no doubt that the country was also different from England, in economic terms, in social structure, and in many political habits and customs. If the linguistic difference was not as deeply marked as between England and Wales, Gaelic was still spoken in much of the Highlands. More importantly, however, religious

11 As well as the specific references which will follow, two works, in particular, are helpful in understanding these questions: W.A. Speck, *Stability and Strife: England, 1714–1760* (Cambridge, MA, 1977); and James L. Clifford, *Man Versus Society in Eighteenth-century Britain: Six Points of View* (Cambridge, 1968). An older interpretation of England, written to ensure an understanding of the country in terms of her eighteenth-century imperial policy, is that of L.H. Gipson, *The British Isles and the American Colonies: Great Britain and Ireland, 1748–1754* (New York, 1958).

belief again differed from that of England. Scottish Presbyterianism was not a very close relative of the Anglican Church.

Finally, one must consider Ireland – the first colonial settlement experiment of both England and Scotland. England's control over Ireland's fortunes, although begun much earlier, was really confirmed by Cromwell in the seventeenth century and the agonies of Wexford and Drogheda during the Civil War. Major Scottish emigration to northern Ireland began in earnest in the early seventeenth century, and in the last decades of that century a major influx of Presbyterian Scots moved across the narrow straits. At the opening of the eighteenth century, Ireland was a poor, bitterly divided land where the majority of people were Roman Catholic, where many still spoke Erse, but where power was essentially still in the hands of the stranger, England.[12] Thus, quite apart from the experience it had gained in colonial matters from its overseas colonies in North America, and from the beginnings of its imperial activities in the Far East, the British government in 1713 had considerable experience in ruling peoples close at home whose mind-set was different from that of its own élite.

Further, if the British Isles, with a total population of approximately 8 million, were something less than the term United Kingdom might suggest, England itself was also diverse enough. But, while distinctions between the South Downs and the Yorkshire Moors, or between the fen country and the Cornish mines, were certainly evident and strong, and even if the divisions between rich and poor were manifest and the contrasts between town and country striking, nevertheless there was a powerful central political consensus throughout the realm. Eighteenth-century England was post-revolutionary. It had the inheritance of the Civil War as well as of the Glorious Revolution of 1688, and it had reached a widely supported consensus on the limits and bounds of many political questions. It could not be called a tolerant society but it was a society that allowed

12 These strangers frequently got their training in the exercise of power in Ireland before moving on to North America. One scholar has noted that "between 1689 and 1727 fifteen or more veterans of William III's Irish war also served as royal governors in Virginia, Gibraltar, Minorca, Jamaica, Barbados, the Leewards Islands, Nova Scotia and Newfoundland and New York and Pennsylvania." Stephen Saunders Webb, "Army and Empire: English Garrison Government in Britain and American, 1569 to 1763," *William and Mary Quarterly* 34 (1977): 15.

tolerance and considered that dissent was possible. It was the society that would soon produce the paradox of the "Loyal Opposition."

In particular, while religious prejudices still affected many political and social decisions, Protestant dissenters and Roman Catholics did not suffer the proscription of their religious practices. While religious conformity was both a government policy and often a social demand, it was not pursued with fire and the sword. Those who did not conform paid for their beliefs politically, socially, and economically, but not with their lives. In 1714 Roman Catholics were legally excluded from public office, from positions in the army and navy, and from seats in Parliament.[13] In France at this time, by contrast, the beliefs of the Huguenots were proscribed, and the practices of the discipline of the Reformed Church was banned by law. There were still eight or nine Roman Catholic peers in England, at a time when the faith of the king was, by law, Anglican.

Thus the absorption of Nova Scotia with its Acadian population into the British empire posed, at first sight, no great or novel problems. London had already coped with people of a different language, the Welsh; people of a different religion, the Irish; and people living at the end of long lines of communications and inclined to riot for their vision of political liberty, the other British North American colonies. However, the particular combination of the specific language and religious beliefs of the Acadians with the political geography of the colony was about to demand flexibility of mind and vision from its new administrators, for the Acadians were on the edge of British imperial territory and linked to another power in that area by language and religion. Throughout the eighteenth century, the problems of imperial security would complicate the British administration of Nova Scotia and the Acadians as much as would the difficulties which naturally arose from the day-to-day life within the colony between its military government and the civilian population.

The selection of military rule for Nova Scotia after 1713 and its basic retention even after 1719, when provisions were made for a civil administration, is not surprising for a number of reasons. First, the colonial authorities had experienced sufficient trouble from what was considered to be New England republicanism not to set about establishing any institutions in Nova Scotia which might give the

13 The number of Catholics increased from about 60,000 in 1710 to around 80,000 in 1770. On this growth see Speck, *Stability and Strife*, 102–4.

population any encouragement to argue with their policies.[14] Second, the system of garrison government, that is, government by military men executing instructions sent them by home authorities was a model well-known to the British by the mid-seventeenth century as Stephen Webb has shown.[15] It seemed particularly appropriate for a colony recently acquired by force of arms. Third, it was very much a continuation of the form of government that the French had imposed upon the Acadians. And finally, while the contemporary interpretation of the laws of England allowed Catholics much social freedom, such laws very definitely controlled the amount of direct political power that could be wielded by Catholics. From many points of view then, military government seemed the obvious choice.

Surprisingly, military government did not lead to any form of rigid military control. Between 1713 and 1730, the Acadians managed to establish considerable rights to the direction of their own affairs. This was due in part to the traditions of independence that they had established even while under French control,[16] and in part to the establishment of a system of representation by delegates. This system had been initiated by Samuel Vetch in 1710 and quickly hardened into accepted practice.[17] From 1713 onwards, any request from

14 For a most useful analysis of the place of New England in the priorities of the Lords of Trade and of the impact of New England activity on the formation of English colonial policy see P.S. Haffenden, *New England in the English Nation, 1689–1713* (Oxford, 1974), especially chapter 7, "Against Port Royal and Quebec: Anglo-Massachusetts Cooperation and the Aftermath of Failure, 1707–1713," 243–90.

15 Stephen S. Webb, *The Governors-General: The English Army and the Definition of Empire, 1569–1681* (Chapel Hill, 1979), 447. For comment on this theory and alternative ideas, see W.A. Speck, "The International and Imperial Context," in Jack P. Greene and J. R. Pole, eds., *Colonial British America: Essays in the New History of the Modern Early Era* (Baltimore, 1984), 389–91.

16 A short account of this is in N.E.S. Griffiths, "The Acadians."

17 Most authorities claim that this was an idea of Samuel Vetch. See for example Brebner, *New England's Outpost*, 62. It was one which the Acadians quickly adapted and made their own. In Mascerene's report of 1714, "[the inhabitants of Minas] desired of me to have the Liberty to choose some particular number of men amongst them who should represent the whole, by reason of the most of the people living scattered far off and not able to attend a considerable time, I easily consented to it and they chose Mr. Peter Melanson and ye four formerly Capts of their Militia with another man for Manis, one for Chicconecto and one for Cobequid." AC, NSA–4, 170.

the British officials at Annapolis Royal (the town of Port Royal had been renamed in honour of Queen Anne) was transmitted to the generality of inhabitants through men chosen by their villages as their representatives. The role of these intermediaries soon became one of spokesmen and nowhere is this better illustrated than with the vexed question of the oath of loyalty. Long letters of comment were sent to the authorities at Annapolis Royal from the villages when requests for the oath were received. When the English officials were actually in the villages, lengthy debates ensued. With these procedures, the Acadians began to develop their own political culture. The role of the deputies was of crucial importance, but there has been very little analysis of what is, in essence, the development of an Acadian political élite.

Oath-taking by subjects in Europe at this time has been studied by Regis Durand.[18] He notes that this procedure was not particularly unusual, especially within the jurisdiction of Great Britain, a power that had recently changed royal families and where Jacobites still protested the Hanoverian succession. What is unusual about the Acadian case is that, over a period of some seventeen years, they were able to negotiate the swearing of an oath that expressed their own particular political wishes. There is no doubt that the British authorities demanded an unequivocal oath of loyalty, in first place to George I, and, on his death, to George II.[19] There is equally no doubt that the Acadians offered, and had accepted by the local officials,[20] a variety of oaths of loyalty between 1719 and 1730, the majority of which contained explicit provisions for neutrality, the right not to bear arms against the French and the Micmac. Neutrality

18 Regis Durand, "L'Acadie et les phénomènes de solidarité et de fidelité au xviie siècle," Etudes Canadiennes 13 (1983): 47–62.

19 The account of this issue by Brebner, New England's Outpost, 70–97 gives the main outlines of the dispute. Documents relating to the issue have been published in T.B. Akins, Selections from the Public Documents of the Province of Nova Scotia (Halifax, 1869); Documents Inedits (Quebec, 1888–91); and Murdoch, A History of Nova Scotia or Acadie, vol. 1.

20 The extent to which these officials misrepresented what was going on to the Lords of Trade is a complex issue. Paul Mascerene, the Huguenot who was to become the Lieutenant-Governor of the colony in 1744 was clear that the Acadians had received some promise to respect their neutrality. See for example "Mascerene to Cornwallis, 1749," in Report Concerning Canadian Archives for the Year 1905, 3 vols. (Ottawa: Public Archives of Canada, 1906), a: App. A, xiv.

was clearly a deliberate policy on the part of the Acadians, of their own devising, and not rooted in either French or priestly councils.[21] Finally, it is also clear that the Acadians had been successful in presenting their own image of themselves to the officials at Annapolis Royal. As Brebner rightly noted, after 1730 "most Englishmen spoke of Acadians as 'the Neutrals' or 'the neutral French.'"[22]

In sum, between 1713 and 1730, the Acadians, with the full support of the British officials, established an effective means of representing the wishes of their villages to these same authorities. As early as 1721, it was clearly established that the settlements had the right to choose their own delegates by means of an annual election,[23] a procedure which a later governor remarked would enable "each in turn [to] share in the fatigue or honor of the office."[24] By 1732 it was acknowledged that the delegates had power to decide disputes about land in their villages, even if, on occasion, their decisions were appealed to the Council in Annapolis Royal.[25] This latter body had been established, in 1719, in order to provide something other than military rule for the colony. It was modelled on the constitution granted Virginia and composed of some ten or twelve men selected by the governor.[26] It was envisaged as something that would initially

21 For a fuller analysis of this see N.E.S. Griffiths, "The Golden Age: Acadian Life, 1713–1748," *Histoire Sociale/Social History* 17 (1984): 21–34.

22 Brebner, *New England's Outpost*, 97.

23 Murdoch, *History of Nova Scotia*, vol. 1, 388.

24 PANS (A.M. MacMechan, ed.), *Nova Scotia Archives II: A Calendar of Two Letter-books and One Commission Book in the Possession of the Government of Nova Scotia* (Halifax, 1900), 89.

25 "As to the letter (to council) ... and the deputies regarding the difficulty of dividing the land between the Depuis and the Claudes, Armstrong can give no further directions. They should divide it at once." Ibid., 81.

26 There is much to discuss about this issue. Brebner, *New England's Outpost*, 134 ff., presents an analysis of some of the difficulties this presented. The first council met in 1720 and consisted of: Richard Philipps, Captain General and Governor-in-Chief, John Doucett, captain; Lawrence Armstrong, major; Paul Mascerene, major; Reverend John Harrison, chaplain; Cyprian Southack, sea captain; Arthur Savage; Hibbert Newton, revenue collector; William Skene, physician; William Shirreff; and Peter Boudre, master of a sloop. Murdoch, *History of Nova Scotia*, vol. 1, 363. See also PANS, *Original Minutes of His Majesty's Council at Annapolis Royal, 1720–1739* (Halifax, 1908), 1.

augment military rule and later develop sufficiently to replace the latter. The Council acted as the Supreme Court of Nova Scotia at this time.

Brebner recognized that the delegates were "in effect the local government bodies of the Acadian population."[27] He was convinced, however, that the Acadians were "not politically minded,"[28] and therefore he did not consider it worthwhile to continue with an analysis of the delegate system as a political framework for the Acadian community. But this system of delegates was not just an administrative convenience. It was a process of crucial importance in Acadian life. Its existence implies a political organization of Acadian life, an organization that was accepted by the colonial authorities and which gave Acadians a voice in the direction of their life within the colony. But it also meant the Acadians accepted that the English officials at Annapolis Royal had a final jurisdiction over a broad area of Acadian life. For example, an argument over the payment of tithes to Father Ignace by the inhabitants of Beaubassin was brought to a Council meeting in late April of 1726. In this case, the Council found for the priest and against the villagers of that year.[29] The same Council meeting also gave judgment over a paternity suit, ordering the reluctant father to pay "three Shillings and Ninepence every Week Until the Child Arrive to the Age of Eight."[30]

While we know very little about the way in which delegates were selected, we do know that there was an elective process set up for the purpose within the communities. The officials at Annapolis Royal appointed an election day and it is obvious that Grand-Pré and Beaubassin did not pick just any adult male when a call came for consultation with the authorities at Annapolis Royal.[31] There must also have been discussion among those involved in the process about what views the delegates should present. The usual differences of opinion within any community about matters of common importance would be the more acute for the Acadians because of their situation as a border people. Their lands were not only currently under dispute by two Empires but had been handed back and forth

---

27 Brebner, New England's Outpost, 149.
28 Ibid., 75.
29 "Meeting of the Council, 20th April, 1726," in PANS, Original Minutes, 111–3.
30 Ibid., 113.
31 On the selection of an election day and problems with the process see the letters of Paul Mascerene to various correspondents from June to September of 1734 in PANS, A Calendar of the Two Letter-books, 140 ff.

between the two as the result of international peace settlements. The French authorities at Louisbourg continuously suggested to the officials at Annapolis Royal and to the Acadians that what had been surrendered at Utrecht was Annapolis Royal itself, which was therefore the only territory legitimately under British control.[32] Acadian policy, expressed by their delegates, would be shaped by the opinion in their communities as to the relative strength of the two competing imperial establishments.

Further, the attitude of the Micmac, neighbours and companions for all the Euroamericans who lived within "Acadia or Nova Scotia," would affect the formation of Acadian attitudes. The Micmac were less than content with the situation that had developed after 1713 and they strove to influence Acadian attitudes towards the English.[33] No more than the Acadians were the Micmac a homogenous, undifferentiated community. Particular bands had their own policies and thus the Acadian leaders had to judge the components of Micmac arguments with as much care as they did the variations of their own Acadian opinion. And this last was a major enterprise, for the central determinant of Acadian life during these years was the extraordinary demographic growth and the related development and expansion not only of formerly established Acadian villages but of new settlements. All these matters would have produced an agenda for a very great deal of debate among the Acadian populace. Inevitably the Acadians evolved ways of discussing and coping with the demands of growth – a system of local government. And the system

32 Where exactly "the ancient limits" of "Acadie or Nova Scotia" ran became more and more crucial as the years passed. By 1748 the English considered they ran from Maine to the St Lawrence river, but the French asserted that they included only half of the present-day peninsula of Nova Scotia, the area around Halifax. After the peace of Aix-la-Chapelle in 1748 there was an international commission set up to study the matter and a flood of books appeared, supporting one side of the argument or the other. See among many Mathieur-Francois Pidansat de Mairobert, *Discussion sommaire sur les anciennes limites de l'Acadie, et sur let stipulations du Traite d'Utrecht, qui y sont relatives* (Paris, 1753); W.M.D. Clarke, *Observations on the late and present conduct of the French, with regard to their encroachments on the British colonies in North America, together with the remarks of the importance of these colonies to Great Britain* (London, 1755); and Anon, *Remarks in ten French memorials concerning the limits of Acadie* (1756).

33 L.F.S. Upton, *Micmac and Colonists: Indian-White Relations in the Maritimes, 1713–1867* (Vancouver, 1979).

of local government of the Acadians, which reached such a visible and important incarnation in the delegates, had a fundamental role in the formation of Acadian culture.

The basis of that culture was the same as that of any expanding colony of Europeans in North America in the early eighteenth century: a society whose populace was flourishing; a community needing and able to provide most of its own basic needs, material and intellectual, from its immediate environment; and a polity in search of effective institutions to ensure the articulation and fulfilment of its beliefs.[34] The evolution of Acadian culture was, however, as idiosyncratic as any other and its distinctiveness is to be found in the intersection of a number of variables.

There is no doubt that by 1730 the Acadians were an expanding population. Governor Philipps, on the second of his two visits to his charge,[35] wrote to the Duke of Newcastle that it was particularly important to secure the allegiance of the Acadians because of "the great increase of those people, who are at this day a formidable body and like Noah's progeny spreading themselves over the face of the province."[36] What is doubtful is precisely what level the population had reached and what role migration played in the increase. The British regime was less statistically minded than the French had been, and the information we have comes from a variety of sources, none of them as full as one would wish.[37] The most considerable settlements were, in ascending estimated numerical order, those

34 The question of colonial identity in Canada has produced and continues to produce considerable debate. See in particular S.F. Wise, "Liberal Consensus or Ideological Battleground" *Historical Papers/Communications Historiques* (Ottawa, 1974): 1–15, R.C. Harris, "Preface," *The Seigneurial System in Early Canada: A Geographical Study* (Montréal, 1984); and Gilles Paquet and Jean-Pierre Wallot, "Nouvelle France/Quebec/Canada: A World of Limited Identities," in Nicholas Canny and Anthony Pagden, eds., *Colonial Identity in the Atlantic World 1500–1800* (Princeton, 1987), 95–114.
35 He held the appointment as governor of Nova Scotia from 1717 to 1749, but was resident in the colony only twice: 1720–23 and 1729–31.
36 Letter partially printed in Akins, *Nova Scotia Documents*, 86.
37 The survival of parish records mirrors the survival of medieval documents: chance as much as anything else has been the deciding factor in the selection of what has survived. As Morris Bishop has remarked: "Truth is more than the record." Other reports on population come from irregular summaries, "guestimates" made for European consumption.

around the Minas Basin, those of Beaubassin, including all of the Chignecto, those of Pisiquid, and the Acadian population of Annapolis Royal coming in last place.[38] It is generally accepted that the Acadian population numbered about 5,000 in 1730. This total implies almost a quintupling of the population in a generation-and-a-half.

Many historians writing about this period have suggested that migration played little or no part in this growth.[39] Yet, as early as 1968, A.H. Clark noted that as far as marriage was concerned, "the records of Grand-Pré show the precise opposite of bucolic isolation."[40] The available parish registers show that partners came into Acadian settlements at Pisiquid and Grand-Pré from Canada, from France, and from Cape Breton Island and the St John river as well.[41]

The caution that Fernand Ouellet has urged about interpreting population data for ideological purposes is worth remembering here.[42] Acadian population statistics have not yet been employed in a debate which sees fertility as French defiance against an Anglophone world. Yet the idea of Acadian identity as founded on a self-perpetuating and genetically exclusive group of families has had considerable influence. The nineteenth-century climate of racism which led minds such as Pascal Poirier's[43] to see familial links with the Micmac as in some way demeaning to the Acadians has an echo in the refusal of certain contemporary writers to acknowledge equally important connections between the Acadians and the English. There is no doubt that, in the early eighteenth century, the majority of Acadian marriages were between people whose families had been settled in Nova Scotia for a generation or more. It is probable, however, that between 25 and 30 percent of the marriages

38 Clark, *Acadia: The Geography of Nova Scotia* (Madison, 1968) 204.

39 Hynes, "Demography," 11.

40 Clark, *Acadia*, 204.

41 The surviving registers for St Jean Baptiste of Port Royal, and St Charles of Grand-Pré are catalogued in NA as MG9, B–8, lots 12(3) and 24(2).

42 The position that Ouellet finds less than acceptable is that which presents the Quebec birthrate as some kind of "défi démographique" against the events of history. F. Ouellet: "L'accroissement naturel de la population catholique québecoise avant 1850: aperçus historiques et quantitatifs," *L'Actualité économique: Revue d'analyses économique* 59, no. 3 (1983).

43 Pascal Poirier, *Origine des Acadiens* (Montreal, 1874).

involved a partner from elsewhere. The influence of these marriages on the life of the settlements and on the relationships between the settlers and the British authorities has not yet been fully analyzed. Yet the marriages between Acadians and the newcomers, marriages which link the descendants of the La Tours, for example, with the new authorities,[44] as well as marriages between less prominent Acadian families and those now considered members of the "English" Annapolis society,[45] meant, at the very least, access to ideas and information of some importance for Acadian politics. Works, such as William Godfrey's elegant and scholarly study of John Bradstreet,[46] one of the children of Agathe de St Etienne de La Tour and an Anglo-Irish officer serving in Annapolis Royal, must be used to describe the social relationships between Acadians and the garrison government and how these affected the development of Acadian policies.

The stereotype of Acadians as a people living in a land isolated from the rest of the world, self-enclosed and inward-looking, inbred and exceptionally fertile, has to yield to the reality of a people with considerable links to communities other than their own, welcoming outsiders into their families, and with a fertility level not significantly greater than that of other Euroamerican communities of the time. In sum, since approximately 25 to 30 percent of recorded Acadian marriages involved a partner from elsewhere, the increase of the Acadian population between 1710 and 1748 was not only the healthy expansion of a self-generating population. It was also a population growth that owed something to the attraction and assimilation of outsiders.

At the same time, however, there is no doubt that there were many marriages among the Acadian families between people of close kin, between individuals whose brothers and sisters, aunts and uncles, had already chosen partners from the same lineage. Trahants very often married Grangers. Blanchards, Leblancs, and Landrys

---

44 Marie Agathe Saint Etienne de la Tour, born in 1690, married, in succession, two English subalterns attached to the garrison at Annapolis Royal, viz. Lieutenant Edmond Bradstreet, and Lieutenant James Campbell. See *DCB*, 2: 590.
45 Such as William Winniett, the Huguenot merchant whose wife was Acadian, *DCB*, 3, 665–6.
46 William G. Godfrey, *John Bradstreet's Quest: Pursuit of Profit and Preferment in Colonial North America* (Waterloo, Ont., 1982).

intermarried.[47] There is also some documentary evidence that can be interpreted to suggest that marriage between second-cousins, which required a religious dispensation, was relatively common.[48] It has to be remembered that the Acadian population of the eighteenth century was very small, even though it was expanding and increasing. On the most optimistic estimate, it only reached 20,000 people on the eve of the deportation. There has been considerable argument over the dominance of the original forty-seven families whose names appear in the 1671 census of the colony.[49] But what is important for present purposes, is the fact that not only were villagers, as often as not, related to one another but that all major settlements had kin-links with one another.

By the opening of the 1730s, the Acadians had become a society with its own developing political culture and were experiencing growth both within established settlements and into new territories. New settlements were established, as in Quebec, mostly by outward migration from older communities. The pattern that Yves Beauregard and fellow researchers have found for New France, that new communities flourished to the extent that they were established by kin groups, people linked by blood and marriage,[50] is very much the pattern that Paul Surette has discovered in his study of the development of Acadian settlement along the Shepody, the Petitcodiac, and the Memramcook.[51] The kinds of forces that Douglas Lamar Jones has written about in his study of migration and society in eighteenth-century Massachusetts,[52] focusing on individual

---

47 The most readily accessible evidence for such links is provided by the work of Milton P. Rieder and Norma Gaudet Rieder, *The Acadians in France*, 2 vols. (1971–2). These books are typescripts of the declarations of lineage made by the Acadians in France after 1763, the original manuscripts being in the Archives d'Ille-et-Vilaine, Rennes; particularly Series C5160.

48 Clark, *Acadia*, 204.

49 Stephen White's work at the Centre d'études acadiennes, Université de Moncton, will provide an answer to this in the near future (see above, chapter 1, n. 33).

50 Yves Beauregard et al., "Famille, Parente et colonisation en Nouvelle France," *Revue historique de l'Amérique française*, 39 (1986): 402.

51 Paul Surette, *Petitcodiac: Colonisation et Destruction, 1731–1755* (Moncton, 1988).

52 Douglas Lamar Jones, *Village and Seaport: Migration and Society in Eighteenth-Century Massachusetts* (Hanover, NH, 1981).

search for fortune and status rather than family exodus to found new communities, seem to have been of less importance for the Acadians.

Expansion, both within the older villages and into the newly claimed lands, meant that matters relating to land titles occasionally took precedence even over the matter of neutrality in the politics of the Acadians. In 1968 Clark wrote: "There is no more vexing question in Acadian historiography that that relating to the circumstances and characteristics of land tenure after 1710. Cloudy as the situation was before, especially on the fringes of Minas, and in Shepody, Pisiquid and Cobequid, it became deeply confused by the ambiguity of the terms of the Treaty of Utrecht and of their interpretation by the Board of Trade or by the governor or his representatives on the spot."[53] In spite of this caveat, both Brebner and Clark spend considerable time and effort sorting out the Acadian system of land-ownership, preparatory to consideration of the link between property ownership and settlement structure. For present purposes, these questions will be looked at as dependent on the position of the Acadians as subjects in a British colony. Leaving aside for the moment the complex debates about the difference between citizen and subject and about the right of the Acadians to emigrate, there is no doubt that from 1713 on the Acadians' right to own land was recognized by the British officials. Evidence for this comes from records of Acadian sales of property and the records of Acadian payments of quit-rents to British officials.[54] Also, the governor or lieutenant-governor in council frequently judged disputes about boundary rights for particular properties, a further recognition of the acceptance of Acadians as land owners in the province.[55] By 1730 the system of delegates had provided the Acadian community with a recognized framework of political institutions. The acknowledgment of Acadians as land-owners by the officials in Annapolis Royal was a further recognition of Acadian legitimacy as a people within the colony.

53 Clark, *Acadia*, 195.
54 On the question of sales see ibid., 195. On the matter of quit-rents see the constant thread of complaint in the Letter-books about the tardy payment of these in PANS, *A Calendar of Two Letter-books*, 81.
55 See in particular Lieutenant-Governor Colonel Armstrong's complaints as to the amount of work this meant in PANS, *A Calendar of Two Letter-books*, 177–8.

In 1730, the Acadians clearly felt their position in Nova Scotia to be secure. It is true that English control over the colony had lasted longer than ever before, that there were more English families within the territory than there had even been before, and that the fishing stations at Canso were dominated by them. Nevertheless, the terms on which they governed the Acadians were no more severe than such terms had been in the time of Crowne and Temple, three generations earlier. The Micmac seemed less contented than they had been, but on the whole Acadian-Micmac relations were peaceful enough. The establishment of French power at Louisbourg did present the Acadians with a continuous reminder of the possibility of battles between great rivals through their lands, but the Acadians knew that Boston smuggled more to that great fortress than they did themselves.[56] While this continued, a major war seemed a remote possibility. All in all, in 1730 the Acadians were not living their lives in preparation for exile: they lived for the development of their society in Nova Scotia. They identified with the land they lived on and bent their energies to the evolution of their own ways of life.

Our knowledge of Acadian society at this time has been obscured by the ways in which the events surrounding the deportation have been recounted. The need to justify the actions of all parties to that tragedy has resulted in the retrospective misrepresentation of the Acadians. They appear as almost anything but a normal community of ordinary humans. Historians and political commentators simplify the realities of Acadian life so that those who are Acadian appear less than human, as either mere puppets of the French[57] or a society of unthinking, innocent victims. Even such an excellent historian as J.B. Brebner subscribed to this latter view, with a belief that the Acadians were apolitical, "scattered farmers," "inhabitants," a community that apparently had no women, no children, no fishermen, no hunters, no traders, no craftspeople. In spite of a great many

56 Trade from New England to Louisbourg in 1740 was valued at 48,447 livres; exports to New England from Louisbourg valued at 70,678 livres. Clark, *Acadia*, 324–5. See also the relevant articles in *Seafaring in Colonial Massachusetts: A conference held by the Colonial Society of Massachusetts Nov. 21 and 22, 1975* (Boston, 1980), in particular Donald F. Chard, "The Price and Profits of Accommodation: Massachusetts-Louisbourg Trade, 1713–1744," 131–52.

57 "They were the victims ... of delusive views that false friends had instilled into their minds." Murdoch, *History of Nova Scotia* (1866), 2: 298.

works which have tried to modify the primary colours of Longfellow's imagination, a vignette of Evangeline in her white cap, strolling with Gabriel through a bucolic setting, still tends to obscure any picture of the many-textured, gritty reality of Acadian life in the 1730s.

There are a number of ways in which one can add depth to the poet's vision, but one of the most important is to distinguish between Acadian settlements. In 1731 Robert Hale, a young doctor, journeyed from New Hampshire to Annapolis Royal and Beaubassin on a sailing ship engaged in transporting coal from present-day Joggins to Charlestown ferry.[58] He remarked that the entrance of the Annapolis Basin was surrounded by "low shrubby Trees" which look "as tho' not one had ever been cut down here since the Creation." There was a cross on a small beach "where the French dry ye fish." He was informed that "French pple." are settled for "30 miles up ye river" and that their settlements were small villages "of about 4, 5, or 6 Houses" set apart from one another by "Small Intervals." Hale's description of the buildings in the Beaubassin area, buildings which included barns and wharfs, chapels, and even an inn, paints a picture of a very different living and working environment. In reconstructing Acadian life at this time one needs concepts that attempt to convey its wide variety of human settlement patterns, ideas about hamlets and bleds, the clachan or the bourg, nouns which describe small collections of dwellings with very few additional outbuildings, whether for agricultural or fishing use, or for religious or other community needs.[59] The Acadian settlements can be compared to small contemporary communities of two or three families scattered within a given area, such as those that ring the Breton coasts or the shores of Cornwall, or those to be found along the Gaspé and down the coast of Maine. The density of settlement that a village implies, some ten to twenty distinct, if inter-related, families is to be found, perhaps, only along the Annapolis Valley, and in the Minas Basin settlements. But where the present-day Sackvilles in New Brunswick now stand, at places such as Westcock and Shepody, the houses did make a community, even if physically it seemed haphazard rather than planned. Hale remarked that he visited the three or four

58 The account of Robert Hale's journey, "A Voyage to Nova Scotia," has been published in the *Historical Collections of the Essex Institute* 42 (1906): 217–43.

59 Pierre Flatres, "Historical Geography of Western France" in H. Clout, ed., *Themes in the Historical Geography of France* (London, 1977), 300–13.

"French houses called Worfcock [Westcock] and the French entertain'd us with much Civility and Courtesy."[60]

Further, the characterization of the Acadians as farmers has rended to obscure the significance of the river valley and the sea in Acadian settlement patterns. In fact the complete absence in Longfellow's poem of the sea as a vital component of Acadian life is one of its conspicuous flaws. There must have been very few Acadians for whom the sea, with all its moods and mysteries, was totally unknown. In 1746 a specifically Acadian vocabulary was compiled. It was a list of maritime words and terms with an explanation of Acadian usage, words such as "appareiller," explained as "se preparer a partir ou mettre a la voile."[61] In her monumental study of the origin and development of Acadian speech, Geneviève Massignon presented a specific analysis of the way in which common nautical terms were employed in Acadian speech for everyday land situations.[62] For example, "le large," the word for the boundless seas, was used very early on to describe the forest, to give an idea of trackless woods. The word "amarre," usually employed for securing boats, was used to refer to tethering animals. The sea, as a source of food, a means of communication, and as a framework for daily living, was a constant companion for most Acadians.

Even in the villages of Grand-Pré, villages whose life styles have usually been recounted as exclusively agricultural, the sea was the support of that very agricultural life. It was the tides that necessitated the dykes that controlled methods of farming. It would be the height of the spring and fall tides, quite as much as the seasonal demands of ploughing, sowing and reaping, that would structure the times of dyke repair and building.

Jean Claude Dupont, in his *Histoire Populaire de l'Acadie*, has emphasized what the location of dwellings on river banks meant for Acadian society.[63] Here the impact of the environment both encouraged and demanded certain adaptions. Estuaries meant shore fishing with nets and weirs. The rivers themselves meant ease of travel, once canoes and skiffs had been built. Here is one of the most important links between Acadian and Micmac. The Acadians adapted Micmac canoes and benefitted from the Micmac knowledge

60 Hale, "A Voyage to Nova Scotia," 231.
61 "Vocabulaire Marin," in *Documents inédits sur le Canada et l'Amerique*, 3 vols. (Paris, 1888), 1: 70–4.
62 Geneviève Massignon, *Les parlers francais d'Acadie*, (Paris, 1955), 2: 733.

of the seas of the Gulf of St Lawrence.[64] Seagoing pursuits, the
hunting of walrus and other fur-bearing animals, added a further
dimension to this aspect of Acadian life, particularly off the shore
from Baie Verte to the Baie de Chaleur.[65]

In sum, the Acadian settlements conformed to the particular environment of the space that surrounded them. The organization of
buildings reflected the landscape, whether it was a sheltered inland
valley, such as that of the meadows behind Annapolis Royal, or the
wild south shore of Cumberland Bay. Similarly, the actual houses
that Acadians lived in varied. Hale noted that the houses around
Beaubassin were all built low "with large Timber and sharp Roof
(not one house being 10 feet to the Eves)." The insides of the houses
that Hale visited "have but one Room ... besides a Cockloft, Cellar
and sometimes a Closet." It is a little confusing to decide quite what
Hale was talking about for he goes on to say that "Their Bedrooms
are made something after the Manner of a Sailor's Cabbin, but
boarded all round about ye bigness of ye Bed except one little hole
on the Foreside, just big eno' to get into it."[66] The ground-floor was
probably a central living-room and kitchen, with some space made
private for the parents. Evidence from later in the eighteenth century
reinforces this account of large single-roomed dwellings as a common enough pattern of Acadian house.[67]

But the archaeological work being done on the upper Belle-Isle
marsh in Annapolis County, Nova Scotia, has already revealed that
at least some Acadians lived in dwellings of proportions that would
be considered comfortable today.[68] Once again, diversity is the norm
throughout the settlements. Present opinion holds that houses near

63 Jean Claude Dupont, *Histoire Populaire de l'Acadie* (Montreal, 1978), 31.
64 One of the best references for this issue is Charles A. Martin, ed., *Les
   Micmacs et la mer* (Montreal, 1986).
65 Aliette Geistdoerfer, *Pêcheurs Acadiens, Pêcheurs Madelinots: Ethnologie
   d'une communauté de pêcheurs* (Quebec, 1987) has some invaluable information about early Acadian fishing activities.
66 Hale, "A voyage to Nova Scotia" 233-4.
67 Anselme Chiasson, "Les vieilles maisons acadiennes," *La Société historique acadienne* 25 (1969): 185.
68 Robert Cunningham and John B. Prince, *Tamped Clay and Saltmarsh
   Hay* (Sackville, NB, 1975), 11. But see also the more recent work reported in Hélène Harbec and Paulette Leversque, eds., *Guide bibliographique de l'Acadie, 1976–1988* (Moncton 1988) 225–9.

Annapolis Royal and on the Grand-Pré marshes would have been built *en colombage*, "a sturdy framework of hewn timbers, mortised, tenoned and pinned with tree-nails."[69] On the marshes around Beausejour, as well as in the Annapolis area, sturdy houses were built in a variation of this technique that combined straight pine or spruce trunks and cross timbers of birch and willow, the whole being packed tight with clay, itself bound with saltmarsh hay. At the mouth of rivers, clay and shells were available, to be crushed into chalk or burnt into lime for building. This allowed further variants of the housing styles developed around Annapolis Royal and along the Minas Basin.

The general pattern of all Acadian settlements appears to have been one of houses spread out over a considerable area, but the configuration of dwellings built between Cape Blomidon and Pizi-quid responded to their particular environment of sea, marsh, and navigable, if tidal, rivers. The clusterings of people in the somehat similar landscape of Beaubassin were shaped in response to the broader possibilities offered by isthmus and the ribs of small hills dividing what were streams rather than rivers. However alike they seem at first glance, the lands that the Acadians dyked around Grand-Pré are a softer, more sheltered environment than the wind-blown salt marshes of the Trantramar, two to three hundred kilo-metres north.

In considering any aspect of Acadian life, it is vital to keep in mind the tension between the constants in all Acadians' experience and the way in which local variations were lived. The political frame-work for all Acadians was the status their lands as a British colony, but the experience of that situation was not the same on the Acadian farms behind the English headquarters of Annapolis Royal as it was on the marshlands of the Chignecto isthmus. In the populous, long-standing communities of Grand-Pré and Minas, settlements made up of two to three hundred families, some priorities of social status affected the marriage patterns. Such considerations would be much less strong in the new settlements composed of four or five families where considerations of consanguinity would have very great force. Thus, the new settlements that were developed along the north shore of the Bay of Fundy, and in the valleys of the Memramcook

69 J. Rudolph Bourque, "Social and Agricultural Aspects of Acadians in New Brunswick," New Brunswick, Research and Development Branch, Historical Resources Administration, (quoted in Harbec and Leversque, *Guide bibliographique*, 11).

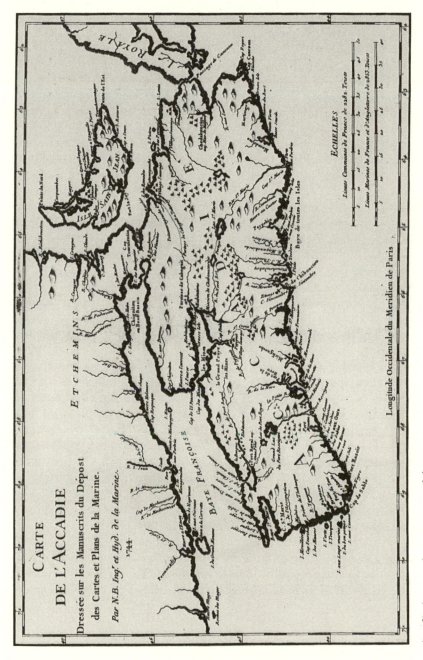

Acadia in 1744 (NA, NMC 19267)

and the Petitcodiac had a pattern of kin relations that resembled those in the older settlements.

Whenever the broad context of Acadian life is considered, it must also be remembered that the individual Acadians lived and died with personal and private experiences. Myriad small choices made up the rich tapestry of Acadian culture. But the common context was crucial. The foundation of survival for men and women in Acadia was no different than it had been for centuries, in Europe and elsewhere. Food, shelter, mental and spiritual nurturance, and emotional stability could be found within a household, most usually a family. Whether lives were lived on the slopes of the Pyrennees or at the mouth of the Petitcodiac, the single life was rare. Even beggars, thieves, and brigands lived in communities, however transitory and shifting the membership. There were hermits and now and again a personage of status and wealth would create a life-style that centered upon that individual alone. The vast majority of people, however, found their lives as part of household community, at the centre of which was a married couple.

The importance and place of children within the family shaped and was shaped by the constant work of both men and women. Sustaining the generations meant changing but never-ending work for both sexes throughout the year. I have never understood how anyone could give credence to the idea that the Acadians were an indolent people, some variation of Tennyson's lotos-eaters. Yet it has been a persistent myth. Putting on one side the comments of officials in charge of the Acadians for either France or England and equally inclined to denigrate the inhabitants, this charge of indolence was often made by visitors too. The French surgeon and writer Diereville crossed the Atlantic in 1699 and recorded his impressions of Acadie at length.[70] His judgement of the Acadians was that

L'oisivite leur plait, ils aiment le repos
De mille soins facheux le pays les delivre.[71]

No more wrong-headed judgment of Acadian society in the early eighteenth century could have been made. Diereville did indeed notice the numbers of children alive and being reared in the settle

---

70 Jacques Rousseau, "Diereville," *DCB*, 2: 188–9.
71 Diereville, *Relations du voyage du Port Royal de l'Acadie ou de la Nouvelle-France*, 2 vols. (Paris, 1708), 2: 255.

ments. He also remarked upon the self-sufficiency of the villages. But he was unable to interpret his observations except through the blinkered vision of his life as a privileged and cultured bachelor – a member of a sophisticated European urban society that had little imaginative understanding of the lives of those who worked the land and drew food from the seas and the forests.

Acadian life demanded something akin to the ethic of nineteenth-century Maine, described by Thomas Hubka as "a pervasive ethic of mutual aid ... so deeply engrained that it assumed a quasi-religious role."[72] Neighbourhood co-operation was integral to Acadian lives, whether the work in question was primarily the occupation of men or of women, or tasks done by both. Whether it was work in the household or on the farms, the work necessary to build houses and to furnish them, or the work involved in weaving, knitting, sewing, and mending; whether it was hunting or the preparation of skins for trade; whether it was child-rearing or a matter of instruction in fishing techniques: mutual aid and co-operation made what would otherwise have been a life of unendurable toil possible and, at times, enjoyable.

The most obvious example of co-operative work within the Acadian communities was in the building, care, and maintenance of the dykes. The techniques of marsh agriculture were part of Acadian life from the very beginning. As early as 1635 colonists who knew something about farming estuaries were specifically sought out for Acadie and their skills recorded in their contracts of migration.[73] France had paid attention to the problems of her own salt marshes since the early decades of the seventeenth century. Louis XIII granted privileges to Pierre Siette of La Rochelle in 1639 for twenty years for draining the marshes and flooded lands of Aunis, Poitou, and Saintonge.[74] These areas of France, according to the work of Massignon, provided the ancestors of roughly 52 percent of the Acadian population of 1707.[75]

72 Thomas C. Hubka, "Farm Family Mutuality: The Mid-Nineteenth-Century Maine Farm Neighbourhood," Peter Benes, ed., *The Farm* (Boston, 1988), 13.

73 Anonyme, "Le Role de St. Jehan," *Memoires de la société généalogique Canadienne française*, 2 (Jan., 1944): 19–30.

74 Hugh D. Clout, "Reclamation of Coastal Marshes," in Clout, ed., *Historical Geography of France* (London, 1977), 198.

75 Massignon, *Les parlers français*, 1: 74. The proportion for Quebec from these areas is estimated at about 30 percent.

While the lands around Annapolis Royal were dyked, it is above all in the settlements of the Minas Basin that great earthworks were constructed to allow for the farming of that immense thousand-acre marsh. Such dykes demanded engineering skill and hard labour as well as a considerable amount of organization for their building. We have an account of the construction of a major dyke in the region of Memramcook in 1775 that gives some idea of the scale of such enterprises.[76] The work force of fifty-eight included almost the entire adult male population then settled along the banks of the Memramcook and the Petitcodiac. They worked twelve days straight, days of between twelve and seventeen hours, before what was constructed was in a shape to withstand the immediate impact of tide and weather. Many of the workers brought their own teams of horse or oxen. The final dyke measured 13.5 metres wide at its base, was 7.2 metres high, and 59 metres long.[77] In considering the toil of men and animals, one must take account of the work necessary to shelter and feed both: food supply and sanitation would be important subsidiary tasks in the enterprise.

The dykes demanded a strong sense of community and not only for the co-operation needed for the construction and maintenance of the dykes.[78] Once built, constant surveillance was required to ensure that any weakening of these barriers against the sea was immediately repaired. Where a dyke crossed lands owned by a number of proprietors, one was named as the "sourd du marais" and made responsible for overseeing the indispensable annual upkeep.[79] The dykes and "aboiteaux"[80] of the Chignecto Isthmus, the Hebert

76 While this is a generation later than the period under discussion, I know of no major technological change which would have effected the construction of such dykes in the intervening forty years. Those who laboured and directed the work were Acadian. F. A. Chiasson, "Accounts of Desbarres," *La societé historique acadienne* 19 (1988): 39–46.

77 Ibid., 40.

78 D.C. Milligan, *Maritime Dykelands: The 350 Year Struggle* (Halifax, 1987); and a special issue of La societé historique acadienne, *Les cahiers* 19 (Jan.-June, 1988).

79 Dupont, *Histoire populaire de l'Acadie*, 310.

80 This word refers to the earth and wood constructions which allowed farmers to control the flow of water to and from the sea. In essence it was a clapper valve, a wooden gate with horizontal hinges, that would let out fresh water when necessary and be forced to close by the incoming tide as a barrier to the salt water. The word is Acadian, being found rarely in French dictionaries and absent from Quebec lexicons.

Valley, and those later built from Baie Verte to Caraquet all differ subtly in both scope and function. Dykes built within river valleys to cope with spring floods were not the same as those built to face the daily onslaughts of the tides in the Bay of Fundy.[81]

A common political framework, a strong web of kin relationships, their similar experiences of home and hamlet – all these are important factors in the emerging sense of Acadian identity. The overwhelming unifying factor for the community during these decades, which drew individual experience into identification with the broad collectivity, was the high standard of living that was achieved. It had to be earned by the sweat of the brow, and the continuous labour of men, women, and children. But the result was the stuff of legend. The food supply was varied and more than adequate. Meat and grain were, except in rare instances, plentiful enough to be exported.[82] Cattle, sheep, pigs, and chickens were all raised. Field crops included wheat, rye, peas, and cabbages. From the time of Diereville's visit in 1699 until that of Captain John Knox in 1757, the wealth of Acadian gardens and orchards was recorded. Diereville remarked on the variety of vegetables grown: beetroots, onions, carrots, chives, shallots, turnips, parsnips and all types of salad.[83] Knox noted more particularly the orchards of apples and pears, cherry and plum trees.[84] Fish was plentiful, game available. Milk was a common drink. Hale recorded a couple of meals in his journal: one evening meal included "Bonyclabber, soop, Sallet, roast Shad, & Bread & Butter." (Bonyclabber is a dish made with buttermilk, and is a form of curds; it sometimes has oatmeal in it). The second menu was "roast Mutton, & got Sauce a Sallet, mixed with Bonyclabber Sweetened with Molasses."[85] Alcohol was available, both imported and smuggled rum, and home-made wine and cider.[86]

81 Dupont, *Histoire populaire*, 310–3.

82 Clark, *Acadia*, 324–5.

83 A recent edition of Diereville's *Voyage a l'Acadie 1699–1700*, first published in Paris in 1708, has been issued by La societé historique acadienne, *Les cahiers* 16 (sept.-dec., 1985). It has an introduction and notes by Melvin Gallant.

84 A.G. Doughty, ed., *An Historical Journal of the Campaigns in North America for the Years 1757, 1758, 1759 and 1760, by Captain John Knox*, 3 vols. (Toronto, 1914–16), 1: 105.

85 Hales, "A Voyage to Nova Scotia," 233.

86 There is a complaint from a visiting ecclesiastic that the Acadians spent too much time in taverns, even during the times for Mass. H. Têtu and C.O. Gagnon, eds. *Mandements, lettres pastorales et circulaires des évèques de Quebec* (1887), 15.

Such a list of foodstuffs did not arrive at the table without effort. There were horses, although it is hard to say how common they were. Acadian travel was most often on foot through the forests, or by canoe and small craft along the shore, so that horses, while useful, were not crucially important. Oxen were as important as horses, because of their strength. Ploughing, sowing, reaping, and grinding were often done by hand, with simple tools. Most of the iron tools that the Acadians had, scythes and rakes, hammers and rims for wheels, were imported from Boston.[87] While there were some grist mills, hand quorns were also used. Most houses had their own ovens as well as open fireplaces. Cultivation of the gardens demanded the fortitude to tolerate the mosquitos and other flying pests.

Cooking involved not only the preparation of meals for the day from fresh ingredients but also the preserving necessary for food in the winter months. The Acadians stored root crops and apples. They often left cabbages in the fields until needed. Large animals were probably killed with the agreement of two or three households, allowing a supply of fresh meat without spoilage. Much was available: nothing without labour.

Death came most frequently at the close of many years of life. Children were reared as well as born. Sweeping epidemics of small-pox, typhoid fever, scarlet fever, cholera, and poliomyelitis were unknown. There was neither famine nor war to take its toll of the community. The collective experience was of low infant mortality and of a community of multiple generations. There is still considerable debate over the size of the average Acadian household. Was a house a dwelling place for more than one family? How often did households contain families of two sisters and their husbands or other combinations of siblings and partners? Were grand-parents peripatetic between the households of their offspring or a stable presence within the household of the eldest child? But these questions of detail pale into insignificance when placed against the larger picture of a human community with the resources to see children born and grow up well nourished, to see women survive child-birth, and to have men vulnerable only to the accidents of their work, not to the deliberate slaughter of battle.

Of course, the Acadians were subject to all the ills that flesh is heir to: knives slipped, ships were sunk, the cold and winter storms

87 The best sources at present for Acadian material history are the publications of Jean Claude Dupont and of Parks Canada. New material is frequently being published, for example, Frederic Landry, *Pêcheurs de Métiers* (Iles de la Madeleine, 1987).

storms could kill. There was systemic crippling of bodies overworked by constant toil, and diseases such as arthritis struck. Further, the richness of the community as a whole did not prevent destitution of some of its members. But there is no doubt that life was pleasant between 1710 (the date of the fall of colony to New England arms) and 1744 (the year troops from Louisbourg brought the Anglo-French conflict to Grand-Pré and to Annapolis). The Acadians experienced what would be remembered as a "Golden Age."

Acadian life during these decades was much more than merely a life of politics and economic security. The Acadians no more lived by bread alone than did any other group of humanity. There was a nascent Acadian cultural life. The weaving and cloth-making skills within the community brought colours to personal apparel and household furnishings. There was music and dancing. An ecclesiastic who complained of too much Acadian drinking in taverns during Sunday Mass also condemned Acadian habits of evening gatherings – "les assemblees nocturnes" – and of their singing "les chansons lascives."[88] Stories and legends were recounted.[89] Toys were made for the children and decorations invented for the tools that the adults most often used. Much of this development of artistic activity took place within the context of Acadian religious belief. The particular importance of Catholicism to Acadians has been left for discussion in the next chapter. There is no doubt, however, that an interpretation of Catholicism helped the Acadians form beliefs about their experiences and was significant in both their collective and private lives. But it is important to see Acadian religious belief as just one strand in a complex identity, not the dominating characteristic of the collectivity.

By the end of the 1730s, the Acadians were the dominant society of Nova Scotia and about to enter upon a generation of rapid growth and development. How strong the Acadian sense of community became was to be demonstrated in the decades of exile, when they rejected assimilation to other cultures.

88 Têtu and Gagnon, *Mandements*, 16.
89 See in particular Antonine Maillet, *Rabelais et les traditions populaires en Acadie* (Quebec, 1971).

CHAPTER THREE

1748–1755: Community Devastated

The main theme of this monograph is that the building and development of Acadian society was a much more complex process than has usually been thought, and that a great deal more investigation is needed about a wide variety of questions of Acadian history. This theme was developed in the first two chapters by the description of the two powerful and contrasting polarities in Acadian life: that of the wider world and that of the Acadian community itself. Much about Acadian society not only links that society to experiences of other societies made up of newcomers to the North American continent but is also a consequence of the very existence of these other societies. Further, the emergence of Acadia is obviously related to the broader story of the European migration to North America, and a good part of Acadian developments can be best understood in the context of North American and European history. At the same time, however, Acadia is neither Quebec nor New England, and Acadian life is not just a transposition of European customs. There is a unique Acadian experience, developed partly because of the particular combination of European migrants who came to the colony, partly because of the very environment of the lands settled, and partly because of the peoples already on the territory claimed, the Micmac and Malecite. Acadian life in the late seventeenth and early eighteenth centuries produced a distinct society. Local conditions produced particular problems which were solved by distinctively Acadian methods.

In many ways, it is inevitable that the impact of the forces outside the small settlements of early Acadia should be seen as being more powerful in the early decades of Acadian history, and the internal strengths of this growing community visibly gain power with its very development. In the period that is the subject of this chapter,

1748–56, however, Acadian history is determined by an almost equal balance of internal and external forces. This most traumatic period of Acadian history, the era of exile and proscription, is an era dominated by a major world war. That the Acadians survived the death and destruction that the world war brought them is due, above all, to the nature of the Acadian community itself. Bitter imperial rivalry between England and France brought the suffering. It was the strength of the Acadians that allowed them to endure the years of deportation, to preserve a measure of social coherence and identity in exile, and to re-root their community, after a generation of turmoil, once again in the Maritimes.

The theme of the complexity of Acadian history – the contention that the Acadians are no simpler than the rest of human kind – is crucial for an understanding of the period 1748–84, the period of this chapter and the following. Much of what is considered general knowledge about the Acadian deportation is more myth than history. Had the Acadians been a society of simple and devout peasantry, who were ignorant victims of imperial policies they were too naive to understand, their community would never have survived the attempt to destroy it between 1755 and 1764.[1] It is important to be clear at the outset that these years really did see a policy, not for the physical extermination of those who were Acadian, but for the eradication of the idea of an Acadian community. Charles Lawrence, lieutenant-governor of Nova Scotia in 1755 and the person who must bear the major responsibility for the policy of the exile and proscription of the Acadians, was quite clear as to what he wanted.[2] He wrote a circular which was dispatched from Halifax on 11 August 1755[3] to inform the other governors of British colonies in North America that the deportation of Acadians was underway. After list

1 The historiographical debate has produced countless volumes, but much of the argument can be found summarised in N.E.S. Griffiths, *The Acadian Deportation: Deliberate Perfidy or Cruel Necessity?* (Toronto, 1969).

2 I should note here that in making this judgment, I am not trying to answer the vexed question of who was responsible for the Acadian deportation. I merely assert that it was Lawrence who accepted the policy as viable though he did not invent it, and who, from 1755 until his death in 1760, initiated and followed through its implementation.

3 "Circular letter from Governor Lawrence to the Governors on the Continent," *Report Concerning Canadian Archives for the Year 1905*, 3 vols. (Ottawa: Public Archives of Canada, 1906), 2: App. B, 15–16.

ing the reasons why he considered the deportation necessary, he stated that, "it was judged a necessary and the only practicable measure to divide them [the Acadians] among the Colonies where they may be of some use, as most of them are healthy strong people; and as they cannot easily collect themselves together again it will be out of their power to do any mischief and they may become profitable and it is possible, in time faithful subjects."

The Acadians were to be exiled from the lands they thought their own, and divided among other British colonial societies in North America where it would be impossible for them to organize themselves as a distinct and separate community. They were to be assimilated within the context of each separate colony, from Massachusetts to Georgia, and become undifferentiated from the majority within each colony, unique as individuals but not as a distinct group. Lawrence had an unsophisticated perception of the unity of the other colonial societies in British North America, and certainly no conception of the individuality of, for example, German settlement groups in Pennsylvania or the Scots-Irish in Connecticut.[4] But his main purpose was clear and his judgment unequivocal: the Acadians must cease to exist as a coherent and separate society and become, in terms of political and civic standing, absorbed into the mass of the other culture.

Surprisingly, Lawrence's ambition failed. While many an individual Acadian perished and many indeed did find themselves assimilated into some other society, an Acadian group identity continued to exist. While there were circumstances in the nature of the exile and proscription which contributed, the continuation of an Acadian identity was largely due to the characteristics that had become the hallmark of Acadian identity before 1755. Any assessment of why exile did not triumph has to start from an appreciation of the nature of the Acadian community before 1755.

The size of Acadian population in 1755 has still not been established, even after the splendid work by Jean Daigle and Robert

4 The literature on colonial British America is both extensive and excellent. However, on this issue see in particular Walter Allen Knittle, *Early Eighteenth Century Palatine Emigration: A British Government Redemptioner Project to Manufacture Naval Stores* (Baltimore, 1970); and N.D. Landsman, *Scotland and Its First American Colony, 1683–1675* (Princeton, 1985) especially chapter 6, "A Scots' Settlement or an English Settlement: Cultural Conflict and the Establishment of Ethnic Identity," 163 ff.

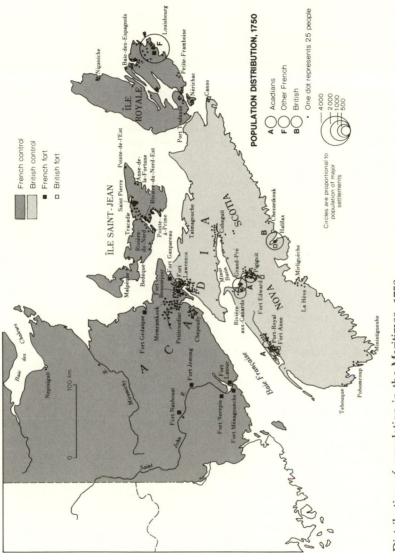

POPULATION DISTRIBUTION, 1750

A ◯ Acadians
F ◯◯◯ Other French
B ◯◯ British
· One dot represents 25 people

4000
2000
1000
500

Circles are proportional to
population of major
settlements

French control
British control
■ French fort
□ British fort

ÎLE SAINT-JEAN

ÎLE ROYALE

NOVA SCOTIA

ACADIA

Baie des Chaleurs
Nepisiguit
Miramichy R.
Fort Gédaïque
Menaramkook
Fort Beauséjour
Fort Lawrence
Petitcoudiac
Chepoudy
Fort Nashouat
St. John R.
Fort Jemseg
Fort Latour
Fort Nerepis
Fort Ménagoueche
Saint
100 km
0

Malpeque
Bedeque
Rivière-du-Nord
Pointe-à-Prime
Fort Gaspareau
Tracadie
Saint Pierre
Anse-de-la-Fortune
Rivière-du-Nord-Est
Pointe-de-l'Est

Niganiche
Baie-des-Espagnols
F Louisbourg
Petite-Framboise
Nérichac
Port Toulouse
Canso

Tatmagouche
Cobeguit
Chezzetkouk
B Halifax
Grand-Pré
A Pigiguit
Fort Edward
Minas Basin
Rivière aux-Canards
Port-Royal
Fort Anne
A
Baie Française
Mirliguèche
La Hève
Teboque
Pobomcoup
Ministigueshe

Distribution of population in the Maritimes, 1750

Leblanc published in the first volume of *The Historical Atlas of Canada*.[5] But disagreement about how many people should be numbered as part of the community that year – 15,000, 18,000, or even 20,000 – is less important than what we do know: the whereabouts of the major concentrations of this population and the main thrust of their expansion.

The older settlements of the Acadian population, those in the neighbourhood of Annapolis Royal, Cape Sable, and La Heve, whose roots are in the 1630s, while significant, are by 1755 much less so than those of the Minas Basin and the Chignecto Isthmus, which were established in the 1670s and 1680s. The Acadian population of Annapolis Royal in 1755 was probably 2,000 and the other settlements – Cape Sable and La Heve – would number at most 400 people.[6] The most populous centers of Acadian life at that time were to be found through the stretch of country from the Minas Basin to the valleys of the Memramcook, the Petitcodiac, and the Shepody. Settlements along the Minas Basin, communities which ran from the base of Blomindon to the gentle hills of what was then called Cobequid (Truro), traced their beginnings back to the 1680s. In 1755 their combined population was in the region of 5,000.[7]

Similarly, the families of Beaubassin, whose houses looked out on the Chignecto Basin from the higher terraces near present-day Amherst and Sackville, lived on land settled at around the same time as the Minas Basin. Bishop St Vallier had visited the area in 1686, finding it a charming region and estimated that 150 people

---

5 Jean Daigle and Robert Leblanc, in R. Cole Harris, ed, *Historical Atlas of Canada: From the Beginning to 1800*, (Toronto, 1987), 1: Plate 30.

6 The French government called for a report on the Acadian settlements in 1748. This is printed in *Le Canada Français*, (1889), 1: 44. It estimates that Port Royal had 2,000 communicants. The original document is in the Archives de la Marine, Paris. I put these figures forward very tentatively. The document of the Archives de la Marine gives 90 families for these settlements, roughly 450 people. My estimate is derived from deportation figures rather than from earlier parish records, and it needs verification. It is interesting to note the extent to which the obvious predominance of the Minas Basin and Chignecto Isthmus has left the Acadian population of these older areas (eg. Port Royal) relatively unexamined by scholars.

7 *Le Canada Français* gives 4,850, which I would accept as a minimum.

lived on the edges of what he described as "un des plus beaux havres du monds."[8] In 1755 the population there was probably 3,000.[9]

The most recently established settlements of the Acadians in 1755 were those of the area known to them as "Trois Rivières": the valleys of Shepody, Petitcodiac, and Memramcook.[10] Small hamlets grew up there from 1731 onwards, when Blanchards, Legers, Dubois, and other families moved out from the Minas Basin, just as earlier members of their families had once moved from the Port Royal settlements to the Minas Basin. The "Trois Rivières" settlement was the most considerable new expansion of Acadian settlement after 1730. By 1755, the population of these river valleys probably totalled between 200 and 300.

While the settlements just enumerated are the most populous of the Acadian community, they represent just that. They are not the totality of the Acadian people in 1755. There were also Acadians settled along the coast from the Baie des Chaleurs to Baie Verte on sites first explored in the 1630s and 1640s, the time of Nicholas Denys and his imaginative enterprises. The most important of these were around the mouth of the Miramichi and at Cocagne and Shediac, also tidewater sites. Further, while there is some dispute as to whether there was year-round settlement by Acadians on the Madeleine Islands at this time, there is ample evidence that these were known and exploited as rich fishing grounds by both Acadian and Micmac.[11] The Acadian interest in Canso should not be overlooked, nor that there were also Acadians along the Saint John River Valley, as far inland as Jemseg. Acadians had settled, along with more recent French migrants, on Ile St Jean and in parts of Ile Royale. Linked by direct kinship ties to people living within the major centres of

---

8 H. Têtu and C.O. Gagnon, eds., *Mandements, lettres pastorales et circulaires des évêques de Quebec* (1887), "Voyage de St. Vallier," 216.

9 *Le Canada Francais* cites 2,500, but the population of the settlements of the Memramcook, the Petitcodiac, and the Shepody areas may be included in that figure.

10 I am much indebted to the recent work on this development by Paul Surette, *Petcoudiac: Colonisation et destruction, 1731–1755* (Moncton, 1988).

11 Aliette Geistdoerfer, *Pêcheurs Acadiens, Pêcheurs Madelinots: Ethnologie d'une communauté de pêcheurs* (Quebec, 1987); Frederic Landry, *Pêcheurs de métier* (Iles de la Madeleine, 1987); and Charles A. Martin, ed., *Les Micmacs et la mer* (Montreal, 1986).

Acadian population, as well as by ties of trade and custom, language, religion and common experience, these people numbered close to 3,000.

The Acadian demographic experience was not that different from the pattern of demographic development elsewhere in colonial North America. The growth of the Acadian population, from roughly 3,000 in 1713 to at least 15,000 in 1755, may have been slightly more rapid than that experienced generally in colonial America, but not overwhelmingly so. Jim Potter has pointed out that "different colonies experienced very different growth rates at different periods."[12] For example, in the eighteenth century the average decennial growth rate in New England was 27 percent. The comparable demographic studies of Acadians have not yet been completed, but it is unlikely that their population growth would be much greater than this.[13] Similarly, the way in which the settlements of the Acadians moved from the Annapolis Basin, along the river valleys and through the marshlands of the Bay of Fundy, as well as to the river mouths along the Atlantic coast, has a striking similarity to patterns of expansion found elsewhere – in Maine and other New England colonies, as well as in Quebec.

The variation of settlement patterns to be found within the colony was much the same as that of New France. Mid-eighteenth century Kamouraska, Quebec City, and Montreal, for example, had as much distinctiveness from each other as they had features in common. Similarly, as has been outlined in the previous chapter, Acadian life in different parts of the territory revealed subtle distinctions between settlements, as well as clear similarities of experience. The Annapolis Valley Acadians had lives dominated by farming, hunting, and fishing, but a fair number of them were connected to the comings and goings of the officials of the small colony. Acadians were pilots for the incoming ships from Europe and, occasionally, part of the tiny bureaucracy.[14] Some pursued commerce and trade, or small-scale home industries in woodwork or textiles.

12 Jim Potter, "Demographic Development and Family Structure," in Jack P. Greene and J.R. Pole, eds., *Colonial British America: Essays in the New History of the Modern Early Era* (Baltimore, 1984), 139.

13 On population rates and their methodology during this period see F. Ouelett, "L'accroissement naturel de la population catholique québecois avant 1850: aperçus historiques et quantitatifs," *L'Actualité économique. Revue d'analyses économique* 59 no. 3 (1983).

14 One was even a clerk to the Justices of the Peace. J.B. Brebner, *New England's Outpost*, (New York, 1927), 150.

The settlers of the Minas Basin had lives which were shaped by dyke-building and an agriculture rich enough to allow for exports, not only to other communities within the colony, but also to Louis-bourg and to Boston.[15] There is some evidence that trade was also carried on with the West Indies.[16] This meant a very different daily round than that of those settled along the Atlantic shore north of Cape Tormentine, or newly arrived on Ile St Jean. The inhabitants of one such outpost, Mirliguesch, were referred by Le Loutre as a mixed collection of "Acadians and ... Savage."[17] Lives in these set-tlements would be dominated by hunting and fishing, with sub-sistence agriculture producing no surplus for trade.

The Acadian society was strengthened, as were the other Euro-pean colonies in North America, by a wide variance of life styles.[18] However, there were a number of significant features which helped to give those who lived in the different settlements of particular colonies a strong sense of common purposes. One of the most im-portant of such unifying factors for the Acadians was external pres-sure arising from the fact that Acadians were considered colonials, and their lands, a colony. While this is true for all European settle-ments in North America at this time, the Acadians had a particularly complex colonial status. A large part of Acadian distinctiveness arose from the impact upon the Acadian polity of the imperial policies of both France and England. The alternating administration of their society by French and English officials, each for considerable pe-riods, helped to produce that mind-set among the Acadians which led them to develope a distinctive policy of neutrality. French and

15 Clark, *Acadia: The Geography of Nova Scotia* (Madison, 1968) 230 ff.
16 Captain Charles Morris, "A Brief Survey of Nova Scotia," NA, MG18, D10, cap. 5, p. 4.
17 "Biographie de Jean-Louis Le Loutre," Archives Departementales de la Vendée, Papiers Lanco, vol. 371, 2.
18 The archaeological work is now being done on Upper Belle Isle marsh, as well as the imaginative work by Azor Vienneau for the film "Premières Terres Acadiennes," will help us to visualise the richness of Acadian life. It will complement work already completed for the Acadian Village on the outskirts of Caraquet. The work of Jean Claude Dupont, *Histoire d'Acadie* (Moncton, 1977) and Dupont, *Histoire Popu-laire de l'Acadie* (Moncton, 1979) needs to be read with an eye to the author's own caution as to the applicability of his information. Time and place are not constant throughout these volumes, and the works need to be read carefully bearing this in mind.

English attempts to control the lands the Acadians settled were accompanied by international boundary commissions and the development of military installations. The founding of Louisbourg and the establishment of Beauséjour by the French were matched by the establishment of Halifax and the organization of Fort Lawrence and Fort Edward by the English. The living space of the Acadians was one of the centres in North America for the conflicting territorial ambitions of two great empires, England and France.

I have suggested elsewhere that one of the keys to understanding the development of Acadian identity is recognizing the reality of their experience as a border people.[19] It is important to realize that the political status of this border varied. In the seventeenth century and until the 1740s, "Acadia or Nova Scotia" was at one of the most important junctions of Anglo-French claims in North America. The colony was a border that made part of the frontier between empires and saw frequent skirmishes which greatly hindered development of the settlements. But, until 1744, "Acadia or Nova Scotia" as a whole was not a battlefield. After 1744, however, the Acadians saw an episode of the war between the Empires involve the heartlands and peripheries of their communities simultaneously. Military historians have noted that by the early 1740s the Missaquash river was the effective boundary between French and English control.[20] It was a boundary that, in the expansion of their communities, the Acadians had ignored when their colony was the meeting place of empires. They continued to ignore it when the colony became the actual battleground of imperial forces.

In the eyes not only of London and Paris but also of officials in New England and New France, Acadia and the Acadians were a disputed resource. Their lands were seen as a legitimate area for control both by London and by Paris. France and England both considered the Acadians' male population as a possible source of military strength.[21] In sum, Acadia was perceived as a colony and

19 N.E.S. Griffiths, *Creation of a People* (Toronto, 1973); and Griffiths, "The Acadians," *DCB*, 4: xxvii–xxxi.

20 George F. Stanley, *New France: The Last Phase, 1744–1760* (Toronto, 1968), 74–5.

21 Their assumptions do not answer our question about Acadian attitudes. Duvivier certainly considered that the neutrality of the Acadians had been responsible for his defeat and lack of success in the expeditions of 1744. See Griffiths, "The Acadians." As far as both British and French policy makers were concerned, however, the Acadian men were seen as a possible military force.

the Acadians as colonials. This is not surprising, for it was partly true. For the Acadians, however, their colonial status was less a central and deciding factor of their political being than it was just another aspect of life, something with which one coped, not something by which one was controlled. Even the system of deputies, a system first structured by the English solely for the purpose of communicating their commands to the scattered settlements,[22] served to reinforce the Acadian sense of their own independence. Over the decades since 1710, the delegates, originally chosen to act as representatives of official direction from Annapolis Royal, became officials themselves. They, not the clergy, became the indispensable arbiters of community life. Occasionally constables and officers of the court at Annapolis, they were more often, as Brebner has summarized it, "registrars-general for their district, [those who] recorded titles, sales, and other transfers, marriage settlements and inheritances, and were regarded by a commission of fifteen percent on the seigneurial fees they collected and small fees for executing deeds."[23] This organization of local government gave the Acadian population considerable experience in self-leadership. We do not know precisely how the delegates were elected by the community, but we do know that they were elected. Thus, before exile, the Acadian people were accustomed to select spokesmen to present their views to others who considered themselves more powerful. This situation could not help but encourage the Acadians to think of themselves having very considerable political rights, even if they were not entirely self-governed.

Further, the Acadian sense of control over their daily lives was enhanced by the fact that, as in most North American colonial settlements, the family was the most important social institution.[24] For the majority of Acadians the family and the household not only formed the basis of their daily experience but also structured their

22 Brebner, *New England's Outpost*, 62 and 149 ff.
23 Ibid., 152.
24 "It is hardly an exaggeration to say that until the late eighteenth century the major social and economic organization in Massachusetts was the family ... Lacking a state bureaucracy, standing army and police force, implementation of state policy depended on the family ... The family was also the centre of economic activity, for there were no banks, insurance companies, corporations or other formal economic organizations." P.D. Hall, "Family Structure and Economic Organization: Massachusetts Merchants, 1700–1850," in T. Hareven, ed., *Family and Kin in Urban Communities, 1700–1930* (New York, 1977), 39.

relationships to the wider community and their working world.[25] Throughout the length and breadth of the Acadian settlements the family and household shaped life for most individuals, whether one looks at the traditional patterns of life on farms in the Annapolis Valley, the mixed trading and farming economies of the Minas basin, or the new ways of life being tried in the Trois Rivières area; or whether one analyses the Beaubassin settlements and considers the out-posts of Acadian life at the mouth of the Miramichi or in Merliguesch. In the two most fundamental aspects of the community, land-holding and religion, family and kin connections played the most significant roles.

To deal with kinship ties first: family relationships within and among the Acadian communities made a close net of interconnections. It was a net, not a solid piece of cloth. Before exile, as afterwards, the Acadians showed a considerable ability to absorb newcomers into their community. As has been pointed out in chapter 2, even in the older settled Acadian parishes of Annapolis, Minas, and Beaubassin, newcomers accounted for a significant percentage of marriage partners.[26] Within a particular Acadian hamlet or village one can find an intricate series of inter-marriages, brothers in one family marrying sisters from another, marriages within the then-forbidden relationship of second-cousin. However, such a pattern of relationships existed alongside families who had no ties to their neighbours, not even by marriage of distant relatives. There has been little comparison of the kin structure of Acadian villages with contemporary villages elsewhere, either in North America or in Europe, and it is not yet possible to say whether the kin lines of Acadian parishes were closer than those to be found in south-western France, in New England, or along the St Lawrence. One can assert, however, that in 1755 Acadian family life was flourishing and as vital to the Acadian sense of community as was family life elsewhere in British North America.

25 The relationship between family and household is one of the most interesting questions being discussed by those working in the field of family history. The work of Michael Mitterauer and Reinhard Sieder – *The European Family Patriarchy to Partnership* (Chicago, 1983) – in disentangling the change from "whole house" to family household leads to a demand for detailed analysis of Acadian kin relationships within a household, as well as for description of ties between households within settlements and from settlement to settlement.

26 Clark, *Acadia*, 203–4.

The Acadian family and household were the economic arbiters of the community, made more powerful because of very lax official control of the Acadians' exploration and settlement of new lands. After 1713 land holdings were granted to individuals directly and Acadians in many settlements paid quit-rents for their property.[27] But the officials at Annapolis Royal and later at Halifax were in no hurry to grant any obviously unchallengeable titles to property since the tenure of land was, as Clark wrote, inextricably linked in the official mind with an unqualified oath of allegiance which the Acadians showed no sign of accepting.[28] The result was predictably chaotic. But land claims by Acadians were registered and suits between Acadians about land were judged by the officials at Annapolis Royal.[29] At the same time, especially in the Trois Rivières region, Acadians, in the words of their own deputies, "[took] possession of and improved large portions of lands"[30] claimed as timberland reserves by the Crown, and ignored any and all demands made by officials to cease and desist. The first settlers in the present-day Dieppe-Moncton region were, as Paul Surette has discovered, two kin groups of families linked by marriage among siblings and cousins.[31] The organization of the plans of these hamlets along the Petitcodiac was not by official survey and land grant: it was by agreement between the pioneers themselves. The Acadian family was the arbiter of plans for new settlements, and it was between kin groups and households that boundaries were claimed and agreed.

27 Lists of quit-rents paid in Grand-Pré and elsewhere in the 1750s can be found in the Brown Manuscripts, "Papers relating to Nova Scotia, 1720–1791," additional Mss. 19071, f. 138–148, British Museum. One of the best analyses of Acadian land-ownership claims is Winthrop Pickard Bell's The "Foreign Protestants" and the Settlement of Nova Scotia (Toronto, 1961), 79 and the footnotes for same, 80–3.

28 Clark, Acadia, 197.

29 See, for example, "Petition of Reny and Francois Leblancs Against Antoin Landry" Council Minutes, Garrison of Annapolis Royal, 7th January, 1731/2, PANS Original Minutes of His Majesty's Council at Annapolis Royal, 1720–1739 (Halifax, 1908), 207.

30 PANS, Nova Scotia Archives II: A Calendar of Two Letter-books and One Commission Book in the Possession of the Government of Nova Scotia (Halifax, 1900) 221.

31 Paul Surette, Petcoudiac, 17. The author defines marriage through male participation, and by so doing overlooks the more complex reality of inter-relationship between households.

As well as being the real authority behind land clearance and distribution, the family was crucial in the maintenance of religious belief. Catholic life gained its daily reality in the practices of the home. Few of the Acadian settlements had resident priests. In 1748, there were five priests reported in action, excluding Le Loutre whose activities were mostly peripatetic and centered upon the Micmac. There was de Miniac, "half blind," de la Goudalie, "quite old and a little deaf," and Desenclaves, who suffered "from a weak chest." This left Chauvreulx and Girard, who were apparently hale and hearty.[32] Basically, each Acadian settlement could count on a visit from a priest annually, and those in the three main regions of Acadian life – the Annapolis Valley, the Minas Basin, and Beaubassin – could also count on a priest residing in the region most years. Weekly Mass was the privilege only of those living within an hour or so's journey of the major parish churches, and priestly blessing of weddings and baptisms took place only when a priest came to a particular neighbourhood. This was a common practice for eighteenth-century Catholicism. A great deal more must be written about Acadian religious practices, based on archival records, including those of the Archdiocese of Quebec, rather than the wishful thinking of nineteenth- and twentieth-century myth makers.[33] It is no slur on the devotion of the Acadians to point out that the rites of the Church were less easily available to them before 1755 than they were after 1830, nor that Acadian interpretation of Catholicism before 1755 was based as much upon individual faith as upon clerically imposed discipline. During the years of exile among mostly Protestant communities of the British colonies in North America, the family framework of Catholic belief proved to be a major factor in Acadian survival.

This crucial importance of family within Acadian society has been unaccountably neglected, given the immense interest in genealogy that has characterised Acadian studies.[34] The archival resources have rarely been examined in detail to discover whether members

32 "Description de l'Acadie avec le nombre des paroisses et le nombre des habitants – 1748," *Le Canada francais*, 1: 44.

33 Micheline Dumont Johnson: *Apôtres ou agitateurs: la France missionaire en Acadie* (Quebec, 1970) makes a good beginning in attempting to assess the influence of the priests on the Acadians during the eighteenth century.

34 This includes the work in progress by Stephen White (see above, chapter 1, n. 33); Placide Gaudet, "Acadian Genealogy and Notes," *Report for 1905*; and Bona Arsenault, *Histoire et genealogie des Acadiens* (Quebec, 1965).

of particular families played consistently dominant roles in the Acadian settlements.[35] Were the Leblancs unusual in being linked to British interests, given the number of men of that name who acted as notaries and delegates throughout the settlements? What would an analysis of land-holding size and numbers of herds and flocks tell us about the economic stratification among the Acadians? The work to answer such questions remains to be done,[36] as does the work to tell what place trading, hunting, and fishing held in each of the Acadian communities at this time.[37] At the moment, one has merely the major outlines of Acadian life on the eve of the deportation. Much of the process of Acadian life has yet to be uncovered.

But even with such a host of questions yet unanswered, it is clear that in 1755 the Acadians were seen as a distinctive society by those who considered themselves their rulers. Sent out by London to govern "Acadia or Nova Scotia" in 1749, Edward Cornwallis informed the delegates who had been brought to meet him that "It appears to me that you think yourselves independent of any government; and you wish to treat with the King as if you were so."[38]

35 Maurice Bosc is undertaking, for an MA at the University of Moncton, a study of marriage alliances which should tell us something of the pattern of social hierarchy among the settlements at this time.

36 While the work demands a painstaking trek through a wide variety of archival holdings, material that suggests patterns of economic holdings is available. The theoretical advances in family studies made by scholars such as John Demos, *Past, Present and Personal: The Family and Life Course in American History* (Oxford, 1986); and Tamara Hareven and Andrejs Plakens, eds., *Family History at the Crossroads: A Journal of Family History Reader* (Princeton, 1987) should be used to provide a clearer understanding of questions concerning Acadian social stratification, the economic activity within households, and the ways in which education, and social welfare are reinforced by political attitudes.

37 We have, for example, documents giving trade at Louisbourg from Acadie in livestock, wood and flour: in 1740 such exports were valued at 26,940 livres, inclusive of some 5,423 livres of furs and skins. New England exports to Louisbourg for the same year were valued at 48,447 livres, including some 4,448 livres of axes and hatchets. J. S. McLennan, *Louisbourg From Its Foundation To Its Fall, 1713–1758* (1918) contains relevant colonial documents outlining this trade.

38 "Minutes of the Council, Wednesday the 6th of October, 1749," T.B. Akins, *Selections from the Public Documents of the Province of Nova Scotia* (Halifax, 1869), 174.

The new governor was right. By the mid-eighteenth century the Acadians did indeed consider themselves a people. Further, they considered that this meant they had definite political rights in society. Acadian policy throughout the years leading up to the deportation was largely based on this conviction that they had, at the very minimum, a negotiating strength in any confrontation with officials, whether military, civil, or clerical, English or French. As late as 10 June 1755, the people of Minas offered to promise "our unshaken fidelity to his Majesty, provided that His Majesty shall allow us the same liberty that he has granted us."[39] This sense of political existence is not without parallel in colonial societies: it is similar to one of the motivating forces behind the American revolution.

It is unlikely that the Acadians ever envisaged exile as a likely fate, even during the tumultuous decade that preceded their deportation. Their tactics were strongly influenced by a belief that the worst that could occur would be a temporary dislocation into French-controlled territory. Ever since 1713 the possibility of Acadian emigration had been part of the rhetoric of political discussion between the English and the Acadians. Such movement had almost always been envisaged in terms of Acadian wish and English opposition. But towards the end of the war of the Austrian succession (usually known in North America as King George's War), the then Lieutenant-Governor of Nova Scotia, Paul Mascarene, reported that there were rumours among the Acadian settlements that "a great force was coming from New England to transport or destroy them."[40] He also reported that every effort was immediately taken to scotch the report. Governor Shirley of Massachusetts[41] issued a proclamation in the fall of 1746 in which he declared

39 Ibid., "Minutes of the Council," 247.
40 "Mascarene to Newcastle, Annapolis Royal, 23rd January 1746-7," *Report for 1905*, 2: App. C, 46.
41 The role of Massachusetts in Nova Scotia history is both important and complex. Brebner in *New England's Outpost* presents a masterly analysis of the relationship from the point of view of imperial policy. George Rawlyk's *Nova Scotia's Massachusetts: A study of Massachusetts – Nova Scotia Relations, 1630 to 1784* (Montreal, 1973) is a complex monograph, centering upon the intricacies of colonial interaction. For present purposes, it is necessary to understand only that, without any hierarchy being stated, the relationship between the colonial administrators of Massachusetts and Nova Scotia was frequently one of senior and junior officials.

in His Majesty's name, that there is not the least foundation for any Apprehensions of His Majesty's intending to remove the said Inhabitants of Nova Scotia from their settlements and Habitations: but that on the contrary it is His Majesty's Resolution to protect and maintain all such of 'em as have adhered to, and shall continue in their Duty and Allegiance to him in the quiet and peaceable Possession of their respective Habitations and Settlements and in the Enjoyment of all their rights and Privileges as his Subjects.[42]

Given the Acadian belief that they had demonstrated their loyalty very adequately in recent years, it would not be surprising for their delegates to consider that their policy of independent neutrality needed no particular adjustment after 1749.

In fact, once open warfare between England and France had been brought to a halt by the treaty of Aix-la-Chapelle in 1748, the relationship between the majority of the Acadian settlements and English officials became much as it had been before fighting gave red snow to Grand-Pré.[43] In 1749, both England and France immediately set about reorganizing their forces and England, in particular, looked to the strengthening of her position in North America. Louisbourg had been returned to France, causing thunderous criticism from Boston.[44] Plans were now made in London to strengthen the British hold on Nova Scotia. A new regime was inaugurated to oversee the foundation of Halifax as well as the establishment of Lunenburg with Protestant migrants.[45] Acadia was to become Nova Scotia, a colony that would be a reliable outpost of the British Empire instead

42 "Enclosure in letter of 20th October, 1747, Mascarene to Newcastle," *Report for 1905*, 2: App. C, 47.

43 Accounts of the impact of the hostilities during the 1740s upon the Acadians abound. One of the best is in R. Rumilly, *Histoire des Acadiens*, (Montreal, 1955), 1: 286–344, but see also G.F. Stanley, *New France*.

44 The most politic expression of these views is contained in "Governor Shirley to the Duke of Bedford, February 18, 1748/9," PRO, NSA, 148–9. For interpretations see Brebner, *New England's Outpost*, 118 ff.; and L.H. Gipson, *The British Empire Before the American Revolution, Zones of International Friction: The Great Lakes Frontier, Canada, The West Indies, India, 1748–1754* (New York, 1942), 5: 180.

45 The work of Winthrop Pickard Bell, *The "Foreign Protestants" and the Settlement of Nova Scotia*, already cited, is a seminal work of meticulous scholarship on this subject.

of a region of doubtful security inhabited by people with question-able loyalty to His Britannic Majesty.

Edward Cornwallis arrived, as has been noted, to take over as governor of the colony on 21 June 1749.[46] While he managed to fulfil a fair number of the aspirations of those who had appointed him, his attempt to make the Acadians take an unqualified oath of loyalty – without any provision for their remaining neutral during an Anglo-French confrontation – was met with a replay of past Acadian re-sponses.[47] On 31 July 1749 the assembled delegates from the Acadian settlements heard Cornwallis proclaim that their position within the colony must be regularized by the swearing of an unqualified oath. On 6 September 1749 the Acadians presented the governor and his council with a petition that requested a renewal of the oath admin-istered to them twenty years earlier by Governor Phillips, an oath which in Acadian eyes had never been repudiated by them nor annulled by the British. Should this petition be denied, the Acadians stated, they would then quit the colony. Cornwallis and his admin-istration made the same response to this reply that their predecessors had done to previous similar rejoinders: inaction. This could be fairly taken as tacit acceptance of the Acadian terms. As Brebner wrote, "the relations between governor and *habitants* had fallen into the old ruts and were wearing them deeper."[48] In these circumstances, it is unlikely that many Acadians envisaged being sent into exile as a distinct possibility even as late as spring 1755. At any rate no alter-ation can be discerned in Acadian attitudes about the oath during the years 1749–55.

However, if the general outlines of Acadian politics towards the English did not change, the converse is not true. Despite the simi-larity of official policy on the question of the oath itself, there were fundamental differences between the regimes of Mascarene and his predecessors and of Edward Cornwallis and his successors. John Bartlett Brebner opened his chapter on these years, which he called "Caught between the duellists," with a striking description of the meeting of Mascerene and five of his councillors with Cornwallis,

46 Murray Beck, "Edward Cornwallis," *DCB*, 4: 168–71.
47 The papers to this exchange are in, *Report for 1905*, 2: App. C, 49 ff. A full analysis of the interchange is given by Brebner, *New England's Outpost*, 181 ff. Brebner's opinion of the Acadians, however, is that they had little sophisticated appreciation of the probable consequences of their actions.
48 Brebner, *New England's Outpost*, 183.

on the deck of HMS *Beaufort* in Chebucto Bay, 12 July 1749.[49] For
Brebner this meeting represented the start of a radically new policy
for the colony, which was "to be prosecuted vigorously and with
generous financial support."[50]

This new policy was a direct consequence of the Treaty of Aix-la-
Chapelle which had been signed in 1748. During negotiations, the
British diplomats had given back Ile Royale and its "great fortress"
of Louisbourg to the French, in return for concessions elsewhere.
Now came London's attempt to redress the balance in British North
America. The policy decided upon had three major features: the
establishment of an English stronghold on the Atlantic coast of the
colony to offset Louisbourg, the general enhancement of the military
presence of the English within centres of Acadian population, and
a scheme for the assisted emigration of Protestants to the colony.
The establishment of Halifax was the most dramatic sign of the new
order. Clark called its building "the greatest public porkbarrel yet
opened in North America" and cited the parliamentary votes for the
construction of the city between 1749 and 1753 as a measure of the
opportunities created. They were "1749, £40,000; 1750, £57,583;
1751, £53,928; 1752, £61,493; 1753, £94616; and 1755, £49,418."[51]
While construction proceeded neither as smoothly nor as swiftly as
its planners had hoped, proceed it did.[52] Despite its reputation as
a place where one-half of the city lived by selling rum to the other,
by 1750 it was asserted that there were 750 brick houses in Halifax.[53]
Its population fluctuated wildly, because it was a port of entry for
new migrants to the colony. Clark estimates that at one point in
1750 there were as many as 6,000 people living about its streets.[54]
Its core population during the period 1749–55 was somewhere in
the region of 3,000.[55] During the early years, many migrants moved

49 Ibid., 166.
50 Ibid.
51 Clark, *Acadia*, 338 and 339 n. 24.
52 There is an account of the first year of Halifax in *Northcliffe Collection,
   Reports* (Ottawa: Public Archives of Canada, 1926), 68–76. See also
   Winthrop Pickard Bell, *The "Foreign Protestants,"* 347 ff .
53 Hugh Davidson, "Description of Conditions [1750] in Nova Scotia," in
   Adam Shortt, V.K., Johnston and Gustave Lanctot, eds., *Documents
   relating to Currency, Exchange and Finance in Nova Scotia with Prefatory
   Documents, 1675–1758* (Ottawa, 1933), 319.
54 Clark, *Acadia*, 338.
55 Thomas B. Akins, "History of Halifax City," *Collections of the Nova Scotia Historical Society* 8 (1895): 3–272.

on to other British colonies. From the outset, however, Halifax attracted a small but steady flow of immigrants from New England. Many opportunists came for the government contract, to sell rum, or to further the smuggling trade between Boston and Louisbourg. Just as many came because they saw a chance for their long-term betterment in the changing circumstances of Nova Scotia. As traders, fishermen, merchants, craftsmen, and even lawyers, they brought a great deal of experience and ability to the new society. At the very least, Halifax gave Cornwallis a strength that no previous English administration in the colony had possessed.

The establishment of Halifax was crucial for the success of the new policy for Nova Scotia, but it was only a part of the scheme evolved by London and Boston.[56] The general strengthening of English military presence throughout the colony that took place at the same time was equally important. The Annapolis garrison was reorganized, and Fort Edward was built at Pisiquid, with a road connecting it to Halifax. In September of 1750, Major Charles Lawrence built a fort, which he named after himself, on the south side of the Misseguash. All these actions brought the reality of the English possession of the colony to the heart of the Acadian settlements in a new and vivid manner.

The third feature of the policy that Cornwallis and his successors pursued was the foundation of Lunenburg and the settlement by 1754 of upwards of 2,000 "Foreign Protestants" there and in the immediately surrounding area. This neighbourhood was that known to the Acadians as Merligash and La Heve. Winthrop Pickard Bell wrote the classic study of this project.[57] He disentangled the mixture of motives that lay behind London's willingness to assist foreign Protestant migration to Nova Scotia at that time and illuminated the complex history of their establishment there. Bell made it clear that after 1749 the officials concerned with these migrants envisaged them as being established in townships of their own. Whatever might have been the dream of Governor Shirley of Massachusetts – that mingling English settlements among the Acadian villages "as contiguous to theirs as maybe" would enhance their loyalty to Great Britain – this vision was no more than advice and advice not followed.[58] Again, as in the case of Halifax, the settling of new migrants proved much more difficult in practice than had been anticipated. But, like Halifax, by 1754 something considerable had been achieved:

56 Rawlyk, *Nova Scotia's Massachusetts*, 190 ff.
57 Winthrop Pickard Bell, *The "Foreign Protestants"*.
58 Ibid., 318.

the foundations of the new community had been laid. The new town of Lunenburg had been laid out, with no concessions made to the steep hillside on which it was built. The grid-iron plan had been used, yielding roughly horizontal streets running parallel to a narrow waterfront and cross streets running at right angles straight up the hill.[59] While the years 1755 to 1763 were hard for these new migrants, in 1754 a settlement was in place, with sawmills in operation, some houses built, some farms laid out, and a number of craftsmen plying their trades.

All this action meant a major change in the political situation of the Acadians. Before 1749, while their lands were the border between two empires, it seemed clear, from an Acadian point of view, that one of these empires, France, was more concerned with the territory than the other. "Acadia or Nova Scotia" could be considered as a distant out-post of the British empire. But it could also be seen as the moving frontier of the French. France had the most impressive military establishment at Louisbourg. Small English trading vessels might ply the waters off the coasts of the colony, but French shipping was more visible. French military action brought war directly into the Acadian settlements in the 1740s. Until the conclusion of hostilities and the fall of Louisbourg, from the Acadian perspective French military force could be considered the more daring and often the more successful. With the foundation of Halifax and the establishment of new forts, this situation was radically altered.

Further, until 1749, it had also seemed clear that Acadian development would set the pattern for the future of the colony. The Acadians had been the clear majority of the population within "Acadia or Nova Scotia" since sometime in the 1720s, when their numbers surpassed the Micmac population. Acadians were the settlers of the colony. Their life-style was its economy. With the arrival of migrants for Halifax and Lunenburg, this no longer seemed obvious. Whilst the English military presence could be dismissed as a temporary phenomenon, the establishment of new villages and towns presaged a more enduring transformation.

If the Acadians seemed to react slowly to these new elements in the life of the colony, the French and the Micmac responded rapidly. As John Reid has pointed out, the French had few grounds on which to object to this outburst of energetic action by the English.[60] But

---

59 Ibid., 426.
60 For one of the most perceptive discussions of events in "Acadia or Nova Scotia" at this time see John G. Reid, *Six Crucial Decades: Times of Change in the History of the Maritimes* (Halifax, 1987), 29–60.

this did not stop an attempt by France to lay *de facto* claim to as much territory in the area as possible. While peace supposedly reigned between the two empires throughout the world as a result of the treaty of 1748, and while an international commission was working to establish the boundaries of "Acadia or Nova Scotia,"[61] the day-to-day life on the frontiers of that colony was punctuated by raid and counter-raid, ambush and seige.[62] Fort Lawrence would soon be faced by Fort Beausejour, whose construction was begun in April 1751 scarcely more than a kilometre from the earlier fortification. In the Anglo-French struggle for dominance in North America, 1748 marked a truce rather than a peace.

The Micmac aided the French by exerting their own pressure on both the English and the Acadians during these years. Throughout the years of the European exploration and settlement of "Acadia or Nova Scotia," the Micmac had never stopped considering themselves the rightful tenants of the land. In 1720 they had affirmed their rights of possession by saying: "This land here that God has given us of which we can be accounted a part as much as the trees are born here .... We are masters independent of everyone and wish to have our country free."[63] The Micmac were not so much allies of the French in the 1750s as they were a people convinced of their autonomy and taking all means to ensure their continued independence. England seemed a greater threat than France to this goal. So the Micmac not only mounted raiding parties against Halifax and Lunenburg, they also helped the French make the Acadian communities of Beaubassin a war zone. In 1750 the Micmac, accompanied and abetted by the French missionary priest, Jean-Louis Le

61 This commission provoked a great many pamphlets, arguing for one viewpoint or another, and a massive collection of documents; but it achieved nothing. However, see *Memoires des Commissaires du Roi et de Ceux de Sa Majeste Britannique* (Paris, 1755); and *Memorials of the English and French Commissaries Concerning the Limits of Nova Scotia* (London, 1755).

62 Stanley, *New France*, gives the most detailed account of this period but A.G. Doughty, *The Acadian Exiles: A Chronicle of the Land of Evangeline* (Toronto, 1916), 72–82 is very clear about the sequence of incidents.

63 "Antoine and Pierre Couaret to Governor Philipps, 2 October 1720," PRO, CO 217/3, f 155–6, cited in L.F.S. Upton, *Micmacs and Colonists: Indian – White Relations in the Maritimes, 1713–1867* (Vancouver, 1972) 199, n. 41.

Loutre, helped to force some Acadian migration from the Beaubassin villages by setting fire to both houses and church.[64]

The extent to which the Acadians remained strictly neutral in these years has been hotly debated. In my view, there is no doubt that the bulk of the Acadians adhered to the policy. There is no evidence of a major rejection of British rule throughout the Acadian settlements. But there is also no doubt in my mind that some Acadians not only traded with Louisbourg and neglected to supply local English garrisons but also supported French activities against the English. There is documentary evidence about the participation of young Acadian men, in particular, in French and Micmac raiding parties.[65] Once more, the key to understanding Acadian action is to consider them as a normal human society, hence as a polity that would contain a variety of views even though a majority would finally unite in support of a common policy. Cornwallis concluded his term of office in August 1752, handing over to Colonel Peregrine Hopson. This latter gentleman only remained in the colony until October 1753, but retained the governorship of the colony until 1755. When he sailed for England, Colonel Charles Lawrence was appointed as lieutenant-governor. Lawrence had had a long career in the military, in the colonial service, and in the colony. He was thirty-eight when he was gazetted major and had joined his regiment in the 1747 occupation of Louisbourg.[66] Whatever one may think of his political abilities, his career shows considerable military perspicacity. There is no doubt that he framed his policies as lieutenant-governor in the light of his military experiences, as will become clear below.

International events are of paramount importance for understanding what happened to Acadian society as Lawrence entered upon his term of office. The new policy introduced by Cornwallis, a policy of increased English interest and presence within the colony, was largely the result of international concerns. It was a policy that prepared for war. It had been framed in the context of a bitter struggle between the English and French colonies in North America. This flamed into open warfare in the spring of 1754 with the clash of the French and American militia in the Ohio Valley. The French were quite as much concerned for boundaries of their empire as were the

64 One of the best accounts of this action is in D.C. Harvey, *The French Regime in Prince Edward Island* (New York, 1970), 137 ff.
65 N.E.S. Griffiths, *The Acadian Deportation*.
66 Dominick Graham, "Charles Lawrence," *DCB*, 3: 361–6.

Eastern Canada in 1756 (NA, NMC 24549)

English and appointed Roland-Michel Barrin de la Galissonière as "commander in chief" of New France. His mission was the "restructuring" of the French empire in North America, a "restructuring" that would necessitate stopping "the undertakings of the English."[67] 1755 was the last year of prologue, the final year of preparatory clash and skirmish the outbreak of world-wide war, a war which would involve battles between France and England not only in North America and Europe but also in Asia. This war became known as the Seven Years War and the peace treaties that brought it to a close in 1763 effectively ended the power of the French empire in North America. In the declaration of war issued from Kensington on 18 May 1756, England put in pride of place the "usurpations and encroachments made by the French upon the English territories and settlements ... in the West Indies and North America ... particularly in the province of Nova Scotia."[68] France issued her declaration from Versailles on 9 June 1756. The events of exile and proscription, which would so profoundly shape the identity of the Acadian community for the next centuries had their immediate cause in the tensions of the New World. Although European men and money were deeply involved in the strategy and tactics of the war effort in North America before 1756, the deportation of the Acadians was, fundamentally, rooted in North American realities and perceptions.

The most obvious of these realities is a matter of political geography: the tactical and strategic possibilities to both sides of the land settled by the Acadians. Moreover, by 1755 "Acadia or Nova Scotia" was not only the border between two rival empires but also in itself a region with considerable tactical importance for both powers.

We have a great deal of information on how Lawrence saw his own policy. There is no doubt that for him military matters were an understood priority. He shaped his policy for the colony accordingly. He wrote, at length, to Governor Shirley of Massachusetts, to other governors of British colonies in North America, and to the authorities in London.[69] Lawrence's policy resulted from the wish to make Nova Scotia a secure and flourishing outpost of the British Empire in North

67 La Galissoniere to the Minister, 25 July 1749. NA C–11–A: 93, 138; on this gentlemen's career see Lionel Groulx: *Roland-Michel Barrin de La Galissoniere 1693–1756* (Toronto, 1970).

68 Cited in B. Murdoch, *A History of Nova Scotia or Acadia*, 2: (Halifax, 1865) 310.

69 Almost all of this correspondence has been printed in Akins, *Nova Scotia Documents*, and *Report for 1905*.

America. He was convinced by 1753, when he was made lieutenant-governor of the colony, that the refusal of the Acadians to take an unqualified oath of loyalty to the British crown made them a major obstacle to the fulfilment of this ambition.[70] He held two completely different, but in his view interdependent, objectives: first, the preservation of British possessions in North America, and, second, the strengthening of Nova Scotia as a crucial and significant part of those possessions.

By the spring of 1755, Lawrence had become thoroughly convinced that his colony could not become a reliable outpost of the British Empire while the Acadians were among its people. Thus the best possible solution was to send them to be assimilated among the populations of the other British North American colonies. In the circular to the governors of these colonies quoted from earlier, this was made plain.[71] Lawrence informed his fellow governors of the unique opportunity now available: "The success that has attended his Majesty's arms in driving the French from the Encroachments they had made in this province," he wrote, "furnished me with a favourable opportunity of reducing the French inhabitants of this Colony to a proper obedience to His Majesty's Government or forcing them to quit the country." He went on to state that "I offered such of them as had not been openly in arms against us, a continuance of the Possession of their lands, if they would take the Oath of Allegiance, unqualified with any Reservation whatsoever." "But this," he also stated, "they have most audaciously as well as unanimously refused." Lawrence therefore turned to the council of the colony "to consider by what means we could with the greatest security and effect rid ourselves of a set of people who would forever have been an obstruction to the intention of settling this Colony and that it was now from their refusal to the Oath absolutely incumbent upon us to remove." The circular continued: "As their numbers amount to near 7000 persons the driving them off with leave to go whither they pleased would have doubtless strengthened Canada

70 "Tho I would be very far from attempting such a step [imposing the unqualified oath] without Yourships approbation, yet I cannot help being of the opinion that it would be much better, if they refuse the oaths, that they were away," in "Lawrence to the Lords of Trade, August 1st, 1754," 55, p. 187 ff., and partially printed *Nova Scotia Archives* 1, 212–14.

71 "Circular letter from Governor Lawrence to the Governors on the Continent," *Report for 1905*, 2: App. B., 15–16.

with so considerable a number of inhabitants; and as they have no cleared land to give them at present, such as able to bear arms must have been immediately employed in annoying this and neighbouring Colonies. To prevent such an inconvenience it was judged a necessary and the only practicable measure to divide them among the Colonies."

Lawrence may have known what he was about and why, but the debate that has raged over the deportation of the Acadians ever since has been bitter and wide-ranging.[72] Whose influence ensured that the proposal of deportation became reality? Governor Shirley of Massachusetts'?[73] What part did London play?[74] Was the determining factor the opinions of the British admirals Boscawen and Mostyn who arrived that spring? Can the whole episode really be summed up, as Guy Fregault believed, as an act of war, and be accepted in that context?[75]

For the Acadians in 1755 such questions must have been of considerably less importance than the events of the dispersion itself. Perhaps the only such matter that would have been argued among them would have concerned their own tactics. The crucial meetings between Acadian and English officials took place in early July, but these meetings were the culmination of an eventful spring. The incident that provided Nova Scotia with the opportunity to deport the Acadians, and to which Lawrence referred in his circular, was the fall of Beausejour, which had capitulated on 16 June 1755. While the campaign to capture the fort had been in progress, efforts had

---

72 See the comments of the Abbé Raynal in his *Histoire philosophique et politique de l'établissement dans les deux Indes* (La Have, 1760), 360. A generation ago there were more than two hundred books and articles in print about the deportation of the Acadians. See the bibliographic guides published by the Centre d'études Acadiennes particularly Helene Harbec and Paulette Leversque eds., *Guide bibliographique de l'Acadie, 1976–1987* (Moncton, 1988).

73 While this has been a favourite conclusion of historians such as Brebner, George Rawlyk hotly contested this judgment in *Nova Scotia's Massachusetts*, 199 ff.

74 On this question see Placide Gaudet, *Le Grand Dérangement* (Ottawa, 1922).

75 "La nouvelle écosse est en guerre et elle s'engage dans un mouvement de colonisation intensive. La dispersion des Acadiens constitute un episode de cette guerre et de ce mouvement." *La Guerre de la Conquête* (Montreal, 1955), 272.

also been made to ensure that the Acadian population, as a whole, would remain quiet. In April and May orders were sent out to the Minas Acadians to surrender not only any weapons they might possess but also their boats.[76] A petition from the Acadians for the return of their possessions was written on 10 June and received in Halifax at the time when Lawrence received the news that Beausejour had fallen and that about 300 Acadians had been found in arms within the fort.[77]

A meeting of the Council, presided over by Lawrence, took place at the Governor's House on 3 July 1755.[78] The petition sent from Minas was discussed with a number of the signatories. The Council took the Acadians point by point through the petition and concluded by asking the Acadians to take an unqualified oath of loyalty to the King. It is obvious from the Minutes of this meeting that the Councillors found the petition "an Insult upon His Majesty's Authority." In it the Acadians had insisted that they had not only not violated their oaths but had kept faithful "in spite of the solicitations and dreadful threats of another power." They had affirmed their intentions of so keeping faith "provided that His Majesty shall allow us the same liberty that we have enjoyed formerly." In sum, the attitude of the Acadians was that they had proved their political neutrality to the government by their past actions and should now be rewarded. The Council was completely unpersuaded by the proofs offered and demanded further assurances. The Acadians, by such phrases as "Permit us, if you please, Sir, to make known the annoying circumstances in which we are placed, to the prejudice of the tranquillity we ought to enjoy," showed that, in their own eyes, they had the right to argue with English officials. The Acadians had held this attitude from the time of François Perrot in 1688. It was a point of view consistently repudiated by those sent from Europe to govern them. It was the attitude that was maintained by all of the Acadian delegates throughout the July meetings of 1755. Polite, unafraid, and obdurate the Acadians offered a qualified oath. The council minutes for 28 July conclude as follows:

As it had been before determined to send all the French Inhabitants out of the Province if they refused to Take the Oaths, nothing now remained to

76 *Le Canada francais*, 1: 138–9.
77 On this episode and its impact on Lawrence see Brebner, *New England's Outpost*, 199–202 and 212–13.
78 Akins, *Nova Scotia Documents*, 247 ff.

be considered but what Measures should be Taken to send them away, and where they should be sent to.[79]

There is one indication that other tactics might have been considered among the Acadians. When finally convinced that exile was imminent, some of the delegates from the Minas basin did offer an unqualified oath of allegiance. The offer was made on 4 July 1754 only to be rejected by Lawrence and the Council on the grounds that "there was no reason to hope their proposed compliance proceeded from an honest Mind and could be esteemed only the Effect of Compulsion and Force."[80]

But such discussions among the Acadians in 1755 would have been overshadowed completely by the events of the deportation itself. The vast majority of the population was shipped away, either in the last six months of 1755 or at some point over the next six years. The last attempt at completing the deportation came in 1763.[81] Those who remained mostly took refuge along the river banks of the Saint John and the Miramichi, or survived more or less as prisoners of war within Nova Scotia. In 1764 Acadians were once more permitted to own land in Nova Scotia.[82] Some 165 families are noted as being in the colony at the time, a population of perhaps a thousand.[83] The size of the pre-deportation population of the Acadians is a matter of considerable debate, with estimates ranging from around 13,000 to more than 18,000. I now consider the second figure to be the more likely. In their work for *The Historical Atlas of Canada*, Jean Daigle and Robert Leblanc present a lower figure, 13,000. They have published the following table of the distribution of the Acadian population at the time of the Peace of Paris in 1763: Massachusetts,

79 "Council Minutes," PANS, RG 5, vol. 187.
80 The issue is discussed extensively by Brebner, *New England's Outpost*, 216 ff.
81 Murdoch, *History of Nova Scotia*, 2: 426.
82 The Lords of Trade were very hesitant about admitting the Acadians as subjects after the Peace of Paris, 1763. However, as of 5 November 1764, Governor Wilmot offered those remaining in Nova Scotia the opportunity to take an oath of allegiance to the British Crown and to be granted land. The correspondence between Wilmot and the Lords Commissioners for Trade and Plantations on this issue is partially published in *Report for 1905*, App. J, 210–16.
83 A report of 1767 estimates the Acadian population of Nova Scotia as 1,265. Ibid., App. L, 255–6.

1,000; Connecticut, 650; New York, 250; Maryland, 810; Pennsylvania, 400; South Carolina, 300; Georgia, 200; Nova Scotia, 1,250; St John river, 100; Louisiana, 300; England, 850; France, 3,500; Quebec, 2,000; Prince Edward Island, 300; Baie des Chaleurs, 700. The total is 12,660.[84]

Again, as with the estimation of the total population of the Acadians in 1755, the numbers can only be taken as approximate, as their authors themselves remark. Questions remain not only about the actual figures, but also about possible groupings of Acadians that have been overlooked: what about the Acadians who had arrived in Santo Domingo?[85] What about the Acadians in the Channel Islands? The more important question, however, is the reconciliation of these statistics with the pre-deportation figures and with the available figures for death tolls among the exiles between 1755 and 1763. Whatever the precise figures may be, there is no doubt that the Acadian community was devastated. The breaking of a people from lands where they had been established for more than three generations was a matter of force and coercion. The Acadians were now officially regarded by the English as a hostile population, whose only rights were to be deported. Lawrence, basing his instructions on work done sometime earlier by surveyor Morris,[86] on 31 July 1755 sent out his explicit directions for the officers who would carry out the operation.[87] There has been considerable debate about whether these instructions show a criminal mind or merely a painstaking administrator at work.[88] The immediate consequence of

84 Jean Daigle and Robert Leblanc, in R. Cole Harris, ed., *Historical Atlas of Canada*, Plate 30. A report to the French government of 1763 estimates the total Acadian population in 1763 as 12,866: some 866 divided among the British sea-ports, some 2,000 in France and 10,000 among the British colonies in North America, *Report for 1905*, 2: App. G, 156.

85 G. Debien, "Les Acadiens à Saint Dominique," in Glenn Conrad, ed., *The Cajuns: Essays on Their History and Culture* (Louisiana, 1978), 255–330.

86 Brown Mss., Add. Mss. 19071–19073, British Museum. There is considerable debate about whether these instructions had been prepared as early as 1751.

87 Printed in toto in the *Northcliffe Collection*, 80–3.

88 For the first view see E. Lauvrière, *La Tragédie D'une Peuple* (Paris, 1922), 1: 465, for the latter, Brebner, *New England's Outpost*, 225. It has been demonstrated for the late twentieth century that these characteristics are not necessarily mutually exclusive.

the instructions being sent was that the military set about their implementation. For the officers who received them, their duty was plain. As John Winslow, the army officer in charge of the removal of the Acadians from the Grand-Pré area, wrote to Lawrence, "altho this is a Disagreeable Part of Duty we are Put Upon I am Sensible it is a Necessary one."[89]

This judgment was the common opinion shared by most of those engaged in carrying out the task. In the words of Major Handfield, the officer in charge of the Annapolis Royal area, it was a "most disagreeable and troublesome part of the Service."[90] But it was policy; the work was to be done. Though Winslow would write to Captain Murray, the officer engaged in the deportation from Fort Edward, that "Things are very heavy on my Harte and hands," he would conclude the sentence, "But as it is shall I question not be able to Skuffell Throh."[91] Once the decision had been taken, the deportation was set in motion and the military carried it out with the inevitable infliction of considerable suffering. But there is no evidence that the cruelty of circumstance was generally augmented by a planned policy of terror.

There was no need for extraordinary measures of brutality to ensure a submissive population. The Acadians were stunned by events. Winslow considered that even when gathered together on the shores, waiting to embark on the transports, the Acadians were not even then fully persuaded that they were "actually to be removed."[92] The reality, even if it had been fully expected, would have been psychologically stunning. Settlements burnt, cattle driven off, lives now entirely at the command of soldiery: within days the Acadians were turned from a free and flourishing people into a crowd of refugees. Winslow has left us an account of the first embarkation from the Minas Basin: his journal reads, "October 8th: began to Embarke the Inhabitants who went of very Solentarily and

---

89 Printed in *Report for 1905*, 2: App. B., 17. John Winslow had been born in Massachusetts in 1703 and at the time of the deportation he was a captain in the British army, stationed in Nova Scotia. He has left a journal of the summer and autumn of 1755 which has been fully printed in *Collections*, Nova Scotia Historical Society, 3: 71 ff. See biography of him by Barry Moody in *DCB*, 4: 774.

90 Major John Handfield to Winslow, 3 September 1755: Boston, MA, Municipal Library.

91 Winslow to Murray, 5 September 1755: *Report for 1905*, 2: App. B., 29.

92 Winslow to Lawrence, 17 September 1755: *Report for 1905*, 2: App. B., 12.

unwillingly, the women in Great Distress Carrying off Their Children in their Arms, Others Carrying their Decrepit Parents in their Carts and all their Goods moving in Great Confusion and appeared a scene of Woe and Distress."[93] This "Woe and Distress" was only the beginning.

The Acadians suffered appalling losses in consequence of the deportation, first on board ship and second on arrival at their various destinations. Shipboard conditions in the eighteenth century were dreadful.[94] Those who sailed with the naval squadron under the command of Admirals Boscawen and Mostyn, which had arrived in Halifax on 28 June 1755, were so severely battered by scurvy, typhus, and yellow fever that they could scarcely manoeuvre the ships into Halifax harbour. The condition of soldiers and sailors arriving at Quebec City in the 1750s was much the same.[95] Conditions for civilians were no better. One traveller of 1734 recorded that passengers were lumped together regardless of sex. He continued, "We were crammed into [this] dark foul place like so many sardines; it was impossible to get into bed without banging our heads and our knees twenty times .... The motion of the vessel would dismantle the apparatus, slinging people into each others' cots."[96]

The circumstances which the exiles experienced were equally as bad, though probably not worse. The condition of the ships putting into Boston, but bound for colonies further south, was reported as bad, the Port authorities remarking that, "The vessels in general are much too crowded; their allowance of Provisions short being 1lb of

---

93　Winslow's Journal in *Collections*, (Nova Scotia Historical Society 1888), 3: 166.

94　"The number of seamen in time of war who died by shipwreck, capture, famine, fire or sword are but inconsiderable in respect to such as are destroyed by the ship diseases and the usual maladies of intemperate climates," wrote Dr James Lind at the beginning of the Seven Years War. The figures for that war bear him out: 133,708 men were lost by disease or desertion, compared with 1,512 killed in Action," N.R.S. Lloyd, *The Health of Seamen* (1965), cited in Christopher Lloyd, *The British Seaman, 1200–1860: A Social Survey* (Paladin, 1968), 234.

95　Gilles Proulx, *Between France and New France: Life Aboard the Tall Sailing Ships* (Toronto, 1984), in particular the tables for sickness of sailors arriving in Quebec, 1755–59, 114.

96　"Rev. Father Nau to Rev. Father Richard, Québec City, 20 October, 1734," *Rapports des Archives de l'Archévêque du Québec, 1926–1927* (Quebec, 1927), 267.

Beef 5lb of Flour & 2lb of Bread prt men [sic] per week and too small a quantity to that allowance to the Ports they are Bound to especially at this season of the year; and their water very bad."[97]

Half of the 415 people shipped on the *Edward Cornwallis*, destination South Carolina, died on route.[98] While this is the largest number of known deaths for one ship, tolls of 20 and 30 percent were not uncommon. At least two of the ships, the *Violet* and *Duke William*, carrying Acadians to Europe, sank with the loss of all on board.[99] Ocean-going travel was hazardous in the eighteenth century, and the Acadians were not spared any of its dangers.

The impact of disease on the Acadians, once they had arrived at their destination, was almost equally devastating. The Acadian communities had relatively little acquaintance with epidemics of smallpox, typhoid, yellow-fever, and other such infectious diseases before exile, and thus no real community immunity to these illnesses. Further, the resistance to infection of those exiled, after the physical conditions of their journeyings, was very weak. The ravages of smallpox, for example, were severe among those who arrived in Pennsylvania.[100] The disease was even more brutal to those who arrived in England by way of Virginia. The death toll was so great, about 25 percent of their number, as to lead to a charge of genocide by France against England.[101]

Causing up to 50 percent death-rates on ship-board, with diseases cutting a further swathe through those who landed among strangers, the actual physical consequences of the deportation of the Acadians sent into exile were ruinous. It must also be remembered that the policy of deportation and exile, begun in 1755, continued until the Peace of Paris. As late as 1762, Jonathan Belcher, who had been the attorney-general of the colony under Lawrence and who succeeded him as lieutenant-governor,[102] was still attempting to deport those Acadians who had somehow escaped earlier efforts. Belcher was

97 *Report for 1905*, 2: App. E, 81.
98 "Report of the Edward Cornwallis," Andrew Sinclair, Master, 17 November 1755; "210 dead, 207 in health," in Council Records (Columbia, SC), 480.
99 Brown Manuscripts, Add. Mss. 19071, British Museum.
100 "Commissioners of the Poor, Report October 1756," in J. MacKinney, ed., *Votes and Proceedings, Pennsylvania*, (Harrisburg, 1931), 6: 4408.
101 Much of this story is covered in N.E.S. Griffiths, "The Acadians of the British Sea-Ports" *Acadiensis* 4 (1976): 67–84.
102 "March 20th 1760, Order-in-Council," PANS, RG 5, vol. A, 70.

convinced that "it will by no means be safe to suffer the Acadians to remain in this Province as settlers,"[103] and so more shiploads of Acadians were sent to Boston in the spring of 1762. That jurisdiction promptly sent them back to Halifax.[104]

Between 1755 and 1762, the majority of the Acadian community that had been built-up throughout the present-day Nova Scotia, New Brunswick, and Prince Edward Island over a course of some 150 years was uprooted. In spite of what became a policy of eradication during these years, some Acadians remained in Nova Scotia at the close of the war in 1763. The Acadian people still existed, they still considered themselves distinct as a community, and they still sought to control their own destiny. As soon as their proscription was ended, in 1764, exiles began to return and rebuild the Acadian community.

103 "Jonathon Belcher to His Excellency Governor Murray, Halifax March 25th, 1762," Report for 1905, 2: App. L, 263.
104 The correspondence on this issue from Belcher to the Board of Trade and also to Lord Egremont, Secretary of State, has been partially printed in Akins, Nova Scotia Documents 329 ff.

CHAPTER FOUR

1755–1784: Exile Surmounted

The years of proscription, from 1755–64, were years of bitter trauma for the Acadian community. They were the years during which the authorities at Halifax attempted to enforce a policy of banishment and exile on all members of the Acadian community. They were the years when the Acadians were dispossessed of all rights to own land within Nova Scotia. The events of these years, whether labelled as "the deportation," "the time of exile," or "le grand dérangement," have become so central to the self-definition of later generations of Acadians that the reality of what actually happened has often been overlooked.[1] Yet the broad outlines of the cataclysm are clear enough. For more than a hundred years, the Acadians had been the dominant society of European descent within the territory covered by the present-day provinces of Nova Scotia, New Brunswick, and Prince Edward Island. In 1755 this pre-eminence was ended, never to be regained. It took more than seventy years for the Acadian population within the Maritimes to reach the level that it had been in the summer months before the boats left. When the numbers once more reached the pre-deportation level of some 20,000 people, the Acadian communities were to be found, geographically, politically and economically, in a very different situation than they had been

---

1 Michel Roy, in his work *L'Acadie Perdue* (Quebec, 1978), 39 considers that the task is both the historian's challenge and the historians' inevitable defeat. Both he and Leon Theriault, the latter in work entitled *La question du pouvoir en Acadie* (Ottawa, 1982), struggle with what the dominance of the idea of the deportation means to Acadian identity today.

in 1755. The policy carried out by Lawrence had both succeeded and failed. It had destroyed Acadian power but not Acadian identity.

Politically after 1755, the Acadian communities would be marginal, if not peripheral, to a majority made-up of several collectivities of newcomers: above all to the Planters and the Scots in Nova Scotia, Cape Breton and Prince Edward Island, and to the Loyalists in New Brunswick. Economically, in the 1780s, the Acadian communities were primarily dependent on subsistence farming, fishing, and the lumber trade. Acadians never regained control of the rich lands of the Annapolis Valley, the Minas Basin, and the largest salt-marsh lands in the world, the Tantramar. Instead, significant Acadian communities were to be found much where they are now: on the northern sea shores of New Brunswick, in the upper Saint John River Valley, around the Petitcodiac and the Memramcook valleys, with a bare scattering of settlements around Cape Breton Island and St Mary's Bay in Nova Scotia, and on the northern shores of Prince Edward Island.[2] From 1755 onwards, the Acadians were a minority where they had once been a majority. They were a community often excluded from the norms of the political life of a broader polity of which they formed part,[3] and their legal rights to establish themselves in certain areas were often successfully challenged.[4] But from 1755 onwards, as in the years leading up to that date, the Acadians lived as a collectivity, as a people with a sense of their distinctiveness, as members of communities with specific and deeply held beliefs in their unique identity. Even when the sense of identity is

2 In 1981, Statistics Canada reported that those with French as a mother tongue made up 5 percent of the population of Prince Edward Island, 4 percent of the population of Nova Scotia, and 34 percent of the population of New Brunswick. Recognition of the Acadians as a French-speaking people with a recognizable community identity encapsulated by the word "Acadian" has not yet been accorded them by the Canadian federal government.

3 N.E.S. Griffiths, "The Acadians," *DCB* 4: xxvii–xxxi.

4 The organization of Acadian settlements after 1764 was controlled by the authorities at Halifax and, later, by those in Fredericton and Charlottetown. There is no question that an Acadian's absolute title to land was often abrogated. On the question of Acadian holdings in the Saint John River Valley see E.C. Wright, *The Loyalists of New Brunswick* (Moncton, 1955).

despairing, a bitter cry of defeat and powerlessness in the face of an uncomprehending majority,[5] an Acadian sense of self endured.

But how did the Acadians survive as a distinct people? What are the connections, other than the purely genealogical, between the pre-deportation Acadian community and later manifestations of Acadian distinctiveness? What is the relationship between the Acadians who returned from exile after 1764 and the shattered remnants of the Acadian society that continued in the Maritimes after 1755, despite every effort of the authorities to complete the banishment of the Acadians. Many of the answers to these questions are to be found in the complexities of what exactly occurred between 1755 and 1763. First and foremost, the Acadian reaction to exile has to be understood. How was it that they did not disappear as a distinct people, that they did not end up by being assimilated into the societies of other British North American colonies or in France? How was it that a significant and important number of them, if by no means the majority, made their way back to Nova Scotia?

But the history of what actually occurred provides only part of the answer to questions of Acadian identity after 1755. A second part of the answer lies in the Acadians' interpretation of the deportation and its aftermath. By the end of the eighteenth century, a shared Acadian belief had evolved about why the deportation had occurred and what it had meant for the Acadian community. This belief was and is crucial for their continued existence as a separate people within New Brunswick, Nova Scotia, and Prince Edward Island. The Acadian history of the exile, as much as the history of the exile itself, needs to be examined. The Acadian interpretation of the deportation became the framework for the development of a rich and distinct identity in the nineteenth and twentieth century.

In the first instance, exile scattered the Acadians into the other British North American colonies from Massachusetts to Georgia. But this was only in the first instance. One of the most important factors which influenced the fate of the Acadians during their exile is that these were years of war. The places of exile were themselves em-

---

5 The poems of Hermenegilde Chiasson are a riveting expression of such emotion, especially those collected in the volume *Mourir à Scoudouc* (Moncton, 1979). It is in his works that one reads: "Comment faire comprendre, faire sentir, faire vivre que l'Acadie ce n'est pas le lèpre que nous ne voulons plus qu'on vienne faire ses bonnes oeuvres parmi nous" 33.

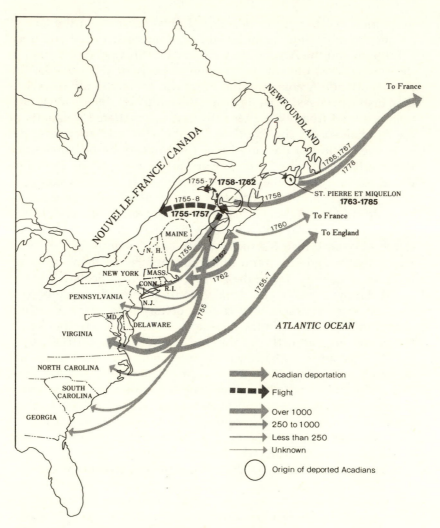

The deportation and flight of Acadians, 1755–1785

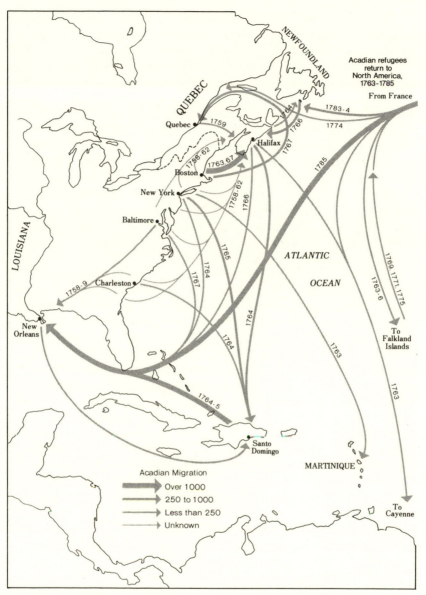

Acadian migration, 1758–1785

broiled, to a greater or lesser extent, in the Anglo-French battle for dominance of North America. What happened to the Acadians immediately on arrival in new lands was often only the beginning of their travails. The Acadians would nowhere find the conditions of their exile stable and unchanging. For many Acadians the deportation meant far-ranging voyages, quite beyond anything imagined by those who had supervised their embarkation in Nova Scotia.

For example, a number of those sent to Maryland, South Carolina, and Georgia went on to Santo Domingo and some of these journeyed to either Louisiana or British Honduras. Others first landed in Massachusetts but after 1763 went to the banks of the St Lawrence. Some voyaged to the Channel Islands and then to the islands of St Pierre and Miquelon. Most of those who were first landed in Virginia were sent on to England and then to France. Many of those who survived this trek sailed from Nantes in 1785 for Louisiana at the expense of Spain, whose territory Louisiana then was.

There is as yet no single-volume history of the Acadian experiences in exile during the years 1755–84, from the deportation to a time when an Acadian community can be considered to have achieved, once more, a legitimacy in the territory, if not on the actual lands, previously settled by their ancestors. There are a considerable number of works which either relate the whole story of some particular group of Acadians or some part of the experiences of most the exiles. Works such as Emile Lauvrière's *La tragédie d'un peuple*[6] give an overview of what occurred. Others, such as O.W. Winzerling's *Acadian Odyssey*,[7] and the more recent work by William Faulkner Rushton,[8] both of which are concerned with the history of how the majority of Acadians that reached Louisiana did so, concentrate on events that only some of the Acadian exiles experienced.[9] Few works have attempted to discuss the available information in order to answer wide-ranging questions about how various jurisdictions dealt

6 Emile Louvrière, *La Tragédie d'un peuple*, subtitled: *Histoire du peuple acadien de ses origines à nos jours* (Paris, 1923).

7 O.W. Winzerling, *Acadian Odyssey*, (Lafayette, 1955).

8 William Faulkner Rushton, *The Cajuns From Acadia to Louisiana* (New York, 1987).

9 The best bibliographic references for this subject are the relevant pages of *Bibliographie acadienne: Liste des Volumes, Brochures et Thèses concernant l'Acadie et les Acadiens des debuts à 1975* (Moncton, n.d.); and Helene Harbec and Paulette Leversque, eds., *Guide bibliographique de l'Acadie, 1976–1987* (Moncton, 1988).

with the Acadians on their arrival or what impact exile had on the Acadian sense of identity. The widely scattered nature of the sources available, both for the North American narrative and for the more far-ranging paths of exile (resources which include the Vatican archives[10] and the graveyards of British Honduras[11]), has understandably tended to encourage the writing of the more restricted accounts of a particular local group. Even the magnificent work of collection which has been undertaken by the Centre d'études acadiennes, at the Université de Moncton, has not yet gathered all known archival deposits. In sum, the history of the Acadians during exile has been recorded either in broad but shallow overviews or narrow but detailed accounts.

The very strength of those incidents of the exile that have entered public knowledge has overshadowed the intricate reality of the exile as a whole, in much the same way as the episode of the deportation itself has thrown so very much of Acadian experience into shadow. Longfellow's poem *Evangeline*, for example, has led many to believe that the deportation of the Acadians entailed the wholesale and deliberate separation of close-knit families, as well as the removal of the whole community directly to Louisiana.[12] The incompatibility of these two ideas is not often noticed. Both remain powerful images of the deportation and both have enough connection with reality to make them enduring myths.

In fact, no one was deported *directly* from Nova Scotia to Louisiana, for, in 1755 Louisiana was Spanish territory and the Acadians were destined for the *British* North American colonies from Massachusetts to Georgia.[13] As noted already, the majority of those Acadians who did reach Louisiana were those who had initially landed in Virginia.[14] There were some Acadians who, having been landed in

10 Archivo Segreto Vaticano, Collegione Nunziatura de Fiandra, 22 November 1763, Leg. 135, which was used by O.W. Winzerling, *Acadian Odyssey: Exile Without End* (Louisiana, 1955).

11 Winzerling notes that he spent several years in the colony where there "were graves of scores of Acadians who had once sought refuge on the shores between Monkey River and Point Diable." Ibid., 70.

12 For a survey of the historical roots of this poem and of the circumstances in which it was written, see N.E.S. Griffiths: "Longfellow's Evangeline: The Birth and Acceptance of a Legend," *Acadiensis* 11 (1982): 28–41.

13 R. Cole Harris, ed., *Historical Atlas of Canada: From the Beginning to 1800*, (Toronto, 1987), 1: Plate 24.

14 Winzerling, *Acadian Odyssey*.

South Carolina, made their way by land to the mouth of Mississippi, although the most used "other route" was via Santo Domingo.[15] The essential plot of Longfellow's poem could have happened and perhaps did. Longfellow heard of the story from an Acadian who was a serving maid, and the legend of lovers parted by the deportation to meet only as death strikes one of them is found in varying forms among several groups of people whose ancestors were Acadian. As suggested already, the years of exile were years of wandering, not years of stability. However inaccurate the detail of incident in the work of this American poet, there is an essential element of truth: the deportation meant the end of a way of life and, for many, the need to construct the pattern of the days in a foreign land.

Similarly, the popular image of the separation of loved ones is both true and false. The break-up of communities was a calculated part of the deportation but, as will be seen in a moment, the separation of closely connected groups was not part of the original plan and was rarely deliberate. As has been noted, when the decision was made to deport, Colonel Lawrence and those associated with him were well aware of the danger of adding to the strength of France in North America. It was for this reason above all that it was decided to split up the various settlements and divide them among the British colonies in North America. To repeat the words of Lawrence again, it was agreed "to divide them [the Acadians] among the Colonies ... and as they cannot easily collect themselves together again it will be out of their power to do any mischief."[16]

Very detailed plans were drawn up to organise the deportation, based largely on the work of surveyor Charles Morris, elaborated by the lieutenant-governor and other members of council.[17] Each major collection of Acadian villages was to be divided up among

15 The best collection of essays on the way in which the Acadians arrived and settled in Louisiana is that edited by Glenn R. Conrad, *The Cajuns: Essays on their history and culture*, The University of Southwestern Louisiana History series no. 11, (Lafayette, LA, 1978).

16 "Circular from Governor Lawrence to the Governors on the continent, Halifax, August 11th, 1755," in *Report Concerning Canadian Archives for the Year 1905*, 3 vols. (Ottawa: Public Archives of Canada, 1906), 2: App. 3, 15–16.

17 Brown Manuscripts, Add. Mss. 190711–73, British Museum. Lawrence's letter of instructions are in *Northcliffe Collection Reports* (Ottawa: Public Archives of Canada, 1926), 80–3.

several colonies. It bears repeating that the Acadians deported from Nova Scotia in 1755, who constituted the vast majority of those sent into exile between 1755 and 1763, *without exception* had as their appointed destination one of the British colonies in North America. The instructions sent to Lieutenant-Colonel Winslow, who would be in charge of the removal of the Acadians from the Grand-Pré, instructed him to ship "To North Carolina ... Five hundred persons or thereabouts ... to Virginia ... one thousand persons; ... To Maryland ... Five hundred persons."[18] Major Handfield, who was in charge of deporting those who were to be removed from the Annapolis Valley, was ordered that the community was to be divided approximately as follows: 300 persons to Philadelphia; 200 persons to New York; 300, to Connecticut; 200, to Boston.[19] The instructions to Colonel Moncton, who was in charge of the Chignecto Isthmus, were to divide those deported as follows: "528 [persons] to Georgia; 1020 to South Carolina and 392 to Philadelphia."[20]

This division of the Acadians can be seen as characteristic of the deportation: it was conceived as a military tactic and designed to mean the end of the Acadian community. It was an act of war. It was not, however, a policy aimed at the extermination of individual; it was not a "Final Solution" bred out of the madness of racial hatred. It was an action comparable to the Highland Clearances. There was no deliberate intention in the plan itself to separate nuclear families, to divide husband and wife, parents and children. In fact, during most of the embarkation proceedings, special efforts were made by Winslow and some of the other officers to bring parents and children together.[21] At the same time, however, there was no attempt to keep the extended family together, as can be seen from cases such as that of René Leblanc, the notary who was landed with his wife and two of his youngest children in New York, with the rest of the family being sent on to Philadelphia.[22]

18 "Instructions for Lieut. Colonel Winslow, Halifax, August 11th, 1755," in T.B. Akins, *Selections from the Public Documents of the Province of Nova Scotia* (Halifax, 1869), 271–4.

19 Ibid., "Instructions to Major Handfield, Halifax, 11th August," 275.

20 "Instructions to Moncton, August 11th, 1755," in *Northcliffe Collection*, 65–7.

21 "Winslow's Journal," *Collections of the Nova Scotia Historical Society* 3 (1883): 97 ff.

22 "Petition to the King of Great Britain, c. 1760," in L. Smith, *Acadia: A Lost Chapter in American History* (Boston, 1884).

But it is important to remark that the plan sketched above was only a plan. It was carried out with all the mishaps and bungling which attend most large-scale human endeavours. Those carrying it out found that it was subject to modification in many detail. Most of the changes increased the distress of the Acadians. Some changes were made because certain of the Acadians proved much more re-calcitrant than had been expected. For example, some eighty-six men who had been held in Fort Lawrence awaiting the arrival of the ships, "got away ... by making a Hole under ground from the Barrack through the South Curtain above thirty feet."[23] Further, as the months passed, Lawrence became impatient and ordered his officers to be more zealous in getting the ships away, and hence to take less account of embarking the men with their families.[24] Yet other changes came about because of the difficulty of organizing and pro-visioning the transports.[25] Perhaps the most devastating changes came because of the weather, which delayed embarkations and then blew many ships from their approved destinations.[26]

The deportation destroyed a way of life and broke a close-knit kin group into fragments, but it was no massacre. Yet limited horror and controlled disaster are horror and disaster nonetheless. Those who survived the voyage often found on disembarkation that their distress had only just begun. The initial separation from neighbours and the break-up of the extended family was often immediately compounded once disembarked. The authorities frequently then split the Acadians into their nuclear families of five to eleven persons in order to ensure that the newcomers would constitute no danger to public order, and to provide for the support of the Acadians according to the norms these polities had evolved for the sustenance of their own sick and poor.

These policies towards the Acadians were adopted in haste by the various colonies. In most cases, the first the new hosts of the Aca-dians knew about the deportation was on the delivery of a letter when a shipload of exiles arrived in the major colonial port, whether

23 "Moncton to Winslow, October 7th, 1755," *Report for 1905*, 2: App. B, 30.
24 "Lawrence to Moncton, September 1755," Vernon-Wager Mss., Li-brary of Congress (Washington, DC).
25 See "Winslow's Journal," vol. 3.
26 The first Acadians to be landed in Boston arrived there as a result of stormy weather. *Report for 1905*, 2: App. E, 81.

that was Boston, Massachusetts; Annapolis, Maryland; Columbia, South Carolina; Savannah, Georgia; or some other port. The captains of the ships on which the exiles left carried a copy of the circular from Lawrence to the "Governors on the continent," dated 11 August 1755. None of the colonies had received any previous official notification, let alone been consulted, about the deportation. Thus, the general pattern of the Acadians' reception was that of an administration having to make some immediate provisions to house and feed unexpected and unwelcome newcomers.

On arrival, therefore, the Acadians were the subject of extensive official discussions and much public scrutiny. They were immediately recognized everywhere as a distinct people: they were unexpected refugees, they spoke French, they were Catholic, and they were in desperate need of succour after the long sea voyage. None of the authorities, whose charge they now were, knew whether to greet them as fellow subjects of the British Crown, removed from a battle zone, prisoners-of-war, "neutrals," or – as Governor Dinwiddie of Virginia wrote to Governor Shirley of Massachusetts – "intestine Enemies."[27] In Pennsylvania the Acadians were considered, and accorded treatment, as "Subjects of Great Britain,"[28] while in South Carolina their treatment wavered between that accorded prisoners-of-war and that which would be given to "natural-born subjects of the Crown" who were yet in need of surveillance.[29] The Acadians were certainly seen as different from those among whom they had been sent to live. And this distinctiveness was further emphasized at the outset by the poor physical condition of the Acadians on arrival. The ill-health of the Acadians meant that the authorities had to intervene decisively and immediately on their behalf. Without exception, all colonies had to set about provisioning the exiles, coping with the impact on them of typhoid and smallpox, and deciding whether they permitted them to land, as did Massa-

27 "Dinwiddie to Shirley, 28th April, 1756," in R. Brooks, ed., "Dinwiddie Papers," *Virginia Historical Society Collections* (Richmond, 1899), 2: 394.

28 Minutes of the Provincial Council, September 1756" *Colonial Records: Minutes of the Provincial Council of Pennsylvania from the Organization of the Termination of the Proprietary Government*, 16 vols., (Harrisburg, Pa., 1852–3), 7: 239–41.

29 28 November 1755: *Extracts from the Journals of the Provincial Congress of South Carolina*, (Charlestown, 1775–6), 513.

chusetts, or to keep them temporarily on board ship, as did Pennsylvania, Virginia, and Georgia.[30]

The debate about what should happen next to the exiles was considerably influenced by how sharply the colony felt the threat of the coming hostilities, for by the fall of 1755 there was no longer any question that a formal declaration of war would very soon regularize the fighting of England and France. If Nova Scotia saw danger in the presence of French-speaking Catholics, the other colonies were equally as aware of the possibility of the Acadians giving aid and comfort to the French cause. The Governors of the differing jurisdictions wrote to one another in great perturbation. Governor Belcher[31] of New Jersey expressed a common view in his letter to Governor Morris of Pennsylvania dated 25 November 1755. "I am, Sir," he wrote, "truly surprised how it wou'd ever enter into the thoughts of those, who had the ordering of the French Neutrals, or rather Traitors and Rebels to the Crown of Great Britain, to direct any of them into these Provinces where we have already too great a number of foreigners for our own good and safety." He was of the opinion that the Acadians "should have been transported already to old France."[32] In Massachusetts, a petition to the governor in February of 1756 complained that about 1,000 Acadians had been landed in the Commonwealth, all in great want and distress, and that "the receiving among us so great a Number of Persons whose gross Bigotry to the Roman Catholick Religion is notorious and whose Loyalty to His Majesty Louis XV is a thing very disagreeable to us."[33] Even in colonies where there was an immediate expression of sympathy for the bereft, there was also wariness and fear. *The Maryland Gazette* of December 1755 remarked: "Sunday Last [Nov 30th] arrived here the last of the vessels from Nova Scotia with

30 Massachusetts: 7 November 1755, Boston State House, Hutchinson Papers, vol. 23; Pennsylvania: "Minutes of the Provincial Council," 6: 712–3; Georgia: George C. Candler, ed., *The Colonial Records of the State of Georgia*, 26 vols. (1904–13), 7: 301 ff.; Virginia: Robert Dinwiddie, *The Official Records of Robert Dinwiddie, Lieutenant-Governor of the Colony of Virginia, 1751–1758*, ed. Robert A. Brock, 2 vols. (Richmond, VA, 1883–84), 2: 269 ff.

31 He was the father of Jonathon Belcher, at that time Chief Justice of Nova Scotia and much involved in the organization of the deportation.

32 Pennsylvania Archives, First Series, 1748–56, 2: 514.

33 Massachusetts State Archives, Council Records, Commonwealth of Massachusetts, 21: 80.

French neutrals for this place, which make four within this fortnight who have brought upwards of 900 of them. As the poor people have been deprived of their settlements in Nova Scotia, and sent here for some very political reason bare and destitute Christian charity, nay common humanity, calls upon everyone according to their ability to lend their help and assistance to these objects of compassion."[34] Considerable concern was also expressed, however, that the Acadians would prove to be spies. The first act which Maryland passed on their account was one in May 1756 to keep them from witnessing any training manoeuvres.[35]

There were some common characteristics in the reception of the Acadians by the governments of the varying colonies on arrival, although the provisions then made for the exiles varied. In general, the exiles were put in the charge of those responsible for the poor of the colony, and distributed, in small groups, throughout the colony in question. As might be expected, colonies north of, and including, Pennsylvania took greater pains to circumscribe the exiles than did the colonies to the south, Maryland, for example, or the Carolinas and Georgia. The actions of the Commonwealth of Massachusetts were followed, to a greater or lesser extent, by Connecticut, New York, and Pennsylvania. A first step taken by the commonwealth was not followed by any other jurisdiction, however. Lawrence was advised, in November 1755, that Massachusetts expected to be reimbursed for any money spent on the Acadians.[36] No other jurisdiction, to my knowledge, took this path. As a second step, the commonwealth passed an act on 16 December 1755 to cope "with divers of the Inhabitants and Families in Nova Scotia ... sent by the Government ... to prevent their suffering by sickness and Famine."[37] By its provisions, a committee was brought into being to organize the immediate supply of food and shelter to the Acadians. Once the immediate needs of the Acadians were met, the

34 Cited in Placide Gaudet, "Acadian Genealogy and Notes," *Report for 1905*, 2: v.

35 Proceedings and Acts of the General Assembly of Maryland (Baltimore, 1930), 24: 461.

36 *Report for 1905*, 2: App. E, 81. Massachusetts nagged at this question throughout the years that Acadians remained a public charge; the final account of £9563 9 shillings and 10 pence was submitted in August 1763, ibid., App. F, 133.

37 *The Acts and Resolves, Public and Private of ... Massachusetts Bay to which are Prefixed the Charters of the Province*, 21 vols. (Boston, 1869–1922), 3: 951.

commonwealth endeavoured to disperse them among various towns and villages of the colony in order that no danger could arise from the exiles gathering together and threatening public safety. Thus, on 27 December 1755, another act was passed which provided for the dispersal of the Acadian families among "several towns" and the binding out of children as servants and apprentices.[38]

There was an immediate outcry against this practice from the Acadians. They organized petitions to Governor Hutchinson, one of which reads in part: "La prève que nous avons souffrir de nos habitations et a mene ici et Nos Separations les Uns les autres n'est Rien a compare a Cell que de prendre Nos Enfans devant nos yex: La Nature meme ne peut souffrir cela."[39] As a result of this and similar petitions,[40] a committee was appointed by the Council of Massachusetts to look into the matter. The report, which they made within two days, and which was concurred in by Council on the day it was presented, recommended that "Selectmen or Overseers should desist binding them out."[41]

The people of Massachusetts, in the words of Doughty, "Loved not Catholics and Frenchmen,"[42] but they were affected by the distress of the Acadians, even though they feared both the expense they would incur on their behalf and the danger that the Acadians might prove to the commonwealth. By June 1756 the roaming of Acadians about Massachusetts, in search of relatives and friends, led to an investigation.[43] On 11 August 1756 an act was proposed "for the better ordering of the late inhabitants of Nova Scotia," which made the penalty for such wanderings "imprisonment and return to their district."[44]

The more time passed the more complicated the problem became.

38 Ibid., 887.
39 Boston State House, *Hutchinson Papers*, vol. 23. This petition is translated and printed in *Report for 1905*, 2: App. E, 88. It is important to consider the original, in which the spelling and grammar indicate that it was most probably written by the Acadians themselves.
40 *Report for 1905*, 2: App. E, 100 ff.
41 13 April 1756, Boston State House, *Hutchinson Papers*, vol. 23. See also Massachusetts State Archives, Council Records, Commonwealth of Massachusetts, 21: passim.
42 A.G. Doughty, *The Acadian Exiles: A Chronicle of the Land of Evangeline* (Toronto, 1916) 184.
43 10 June 1756, Boston State House, *Hutchinson Papers*, vol. 23.
44 Boston State House, *Hutchinson Papers*, vol. 23. Gaudet, "Acadian Genealogy," *Report for 1905*, 2: 89 has the Act as 28–30 August 1756. *Acts and Resolves ... Massachusetts Bay*, 3: 986.

By mid-summer 1756, Massachusetts had not only to cope with those Acadians who had been directly sent to her shores but also had news that "ninety of the French inhabitants of Nova Scotia having coasted along shore from Georgia and South Carolina ... had put into harbour in the southern part of this province."[45] An attempt was made to put an end to such voyagings, as well as to the comings and goings of Acadians within the commonwealth. The records show remarkably little success. Repeated acts and resolutions of the colony's administration reveal a continuing problem, part of it caused by humanitarian reactions. Some voyagings were permitted as Acadian petitions to be allowed to join with relatives were granted.[46] In January, Dedham's answer to a request as to the whereabouts of the Acadians ends with the sentence: "There is another girl who is sometimes here and sometimes not."[47]

On 13 August 1757 the commonwealth made yet another effort to deal directly with the security problem posed by the Acadians who wandered their towns and villages. A circular was issued to all sheriffs, under-sheriffs or deputies, pointing out that "there may be great Danger in allowing the French people, late Inhabitants of Nova Scotia, too great a Liberty at this critical Juncture."[48] But nothing really changed. In 1759, General Wolfe was complaining that "some of the said Nova Scotians have deserted the Province and gone to Canada,"[49] and he demanded a closer surveillance of them. As a result, one more survey was undertaken which reported as follows:[50]

January 25th, 1760:

Acadians able to Labour	304
Incapable by reasons of old age, 50 and up	61
Incapable by reasons of Sickness	107
Children under 7	240
Children capable of being put out from 7 to 14	187
Employed in attending and nursing sick	28
	947 [sic]

45 23 July 1756, Boston State House, Hutchinson Papers, vol. 23. Much of the documentation of this episode is printed in Akins, *Nova Scotia Documents* 302 ff.

46 A good collection of these can be found in *Report for 1905*, 2: 104 ff.

47 Boston State House, Hutchinson Papers, vol. 23.

48 *Report for 1905*, 2: 114.

49 5 October 1759, *Acts and Resolves ... Massachusetts Bay*, 4: 102.

50 Massachusetts State Archives, Council Records, Commonwealth of Massachusetts, 23: 210.

As was to be expected, considering the resolution that had been made when the Acadians first arrived, Massachusetts kept accounts of the cost of their support. For the year 1759 it was calculated as £1478 2s. 9d. Over the years more than one community complained, as did Salem, that "by reason of this addition of Neutrals, the poor of our Town are kept out of the almshouse."[51] The sort of support that the Acadians received is typified by the records of Medway, which spent £711s. 3d. to support nine people from 28 October 1756 to 7 March 1757. The full report reads as follows:[52]

	£	s	d
To House Rent for One Family from October 28th, 1756 to March 7th, 1757		2	8
To nine Bushels of rye meal	1	10	
To nine Bushels and one half of Indian meal and corn	1	2	9½
To 286 pounds of Beef	1	18	1½
To 64 pounds of Pork		8	6½
To 32 pounds of cheese		5	9
To 3 pounds of Butter		1	10
To 8 pounds of Mutton		1	1
To 10 gallons of milk		4	6
To 13 loads of wood		13	
To half a bushel and a peck of Salt		1	9
To Bread			4
To five gallons of Cyder		1	2½
To 2 pounds of wool		4	8
To mending a pot			8
To a wheel and an Axe		16	8
To Mr. John Thibault for Trouble as an Interpreter			8
	7	11 [sic]	3

The nine persons above mentioned the head of the family ... aged 53, his wife 48, they are not well and healthy, not capable of constant labour; their eldest son aged 28, his wife, 23, well and healthy, the next son aged 20 and healthy, the next son aged 16 has been poor and weakly, the next aged 13, next aged 9, the youngest son aged 6, the four last mentioned are small and not capable of doing much for their support. The men are all fishermen. They can handle an axe But do not understand our common husbandry; By reason thereof we can't find 'em Constant Labour.

51 15 January 1757, Boston State House, Hutchinson Papers, vol. 23.
52 (no day given) March 1757, ibid.

The final bill for the monies spent by Massachusetts for the support of the Acadians was computed in September of 1762 as £6,000 and by August of 1763 as £9,563 9s. 10d.[53]. As far as I know, these accounts were never paid.

But while the archives of Massachusetts are full of evidence concerning the expenditures of the commonwealth on the Acadians, that is really the least part of the matter. The decision to deport the Acadians might have seemed a swift and simple solution to a long-standing and thorny problem to the Governor's Council in Halifax in 1755, but its outcome was an exacerbation difficulties for other British colonial administrations in North America and a calvary for the Acadians. In truth, the deportation was a matter of perplexity and confusion for the officials of the colonies to which they were sent, as much as for the Acadians themselves. Further, all involved would find that the repercussions of the policy did not end with Peace of Paris in 1763. In January 1764, Bernard, then Governor of Massachusetts, wrote to the House of Representatives, on the occasion of an epidemic of small-pox in the colony:[54] "The case of these people [the Acadians] is truly deplorable. They have none of them had the small-pox and they depend upon their daily labour for their bread. If they don't go about town they must starve; if they do go about they contract the distemper, and as they are crowded in small apartments and wanting the necessaries of life, they must have a common chance to escape perishing ... I am therefore obliged to apply to you to help to save these people." Some measures were taken to lessen the misery of the Acadians, but their circumstances continued to be pitiable.[55]

In the summer of 1764 there seemed to be a possibility for a new and better life for the exiles, albeit in very foreign circumstances. An invitation was made "to all the Acadians residing in New England" to go to Santo Domingo where they "shall have grants of land made to them and they shall be maintained by the King [Louis XVI] during the first months of their abode."[56] Bernard was much against this. In January of 1765, he sent a message to the House of Representatives that he had been informed that "the Acadians belonging to this province were going hence in large numbers

53 6 September 1762, *Acts and Resolves ... Massachusetts Bay*, 5: 104; and *Report for 1905*, 2: App. F, 133–4.

54 18 January 1764, *Report for 1905*, 2: App. E, 90.

55 A somewhat muddled, but exhaustive account of this can be found in Pierre Belliveau, *French Neutrals in Massachusetts* (Boston 1972), 22 ff.

56 *Report for 1905*, 2: App. E, 90.

to form a settlement in French Hispaniola." He continued: "Their case is truly pitiable; if they go to Hispaniola they run into certain destruction very few escaping with life, the Effects of the bad climate there and yet they have no Encouragement in this Country; Humanity more than Policy makes me desirous to prevent the remainder of them taking this fateful voyage; I want not so much to make them British subjects as to keep them from perishing."[57]

At least some Acadians reacted bitterly to this well-meant paternalism. They informed the governor that "for nine years we have lived in hopes of joining our Country men and it seems to us that you have caused a door which was open to be shut upon us. We have always understood that in times of Peace and in all countries the prison doors are open to Prisoners. It is therefore astonishing to us, Sir, to be detained here ... This is very hard upon us. It is hard to reflect upon our Present situation, to see ourselves by one sudden blow rendered incapable of affording ourselves relief."[58] The governor's desires, however, prevented them leaving.

One scheme might have been thwarted, but another avenue opened. In the spring of 1766 Governor Murray of Quebec wrote to Governor Bernard suggesting that under certain circumstances the Acadians might be settled in his province "for the Good of the British Empire."[59] By 2 June, some 890 Acadians had agreed to be transported to the banks of the St Lawrence. The *Quebec Gazette* of 1 September 1766 reported the arrival of a sloop from Boston with "forty Acadians who, for the Benefit of their Religion, are come here to settle." On Monday 8 September, 1766 "At the Council Chamber in the Castle of St. Louis in the City of Quebec"[60] an order was given to provide one month's supplies to some ninety Acadians, men, women and children.

After this date, information in Massachusetts archives about the Acadians dwindles. In 1766, eleven years after the first Acadian exiles arrive in Boston harbour, noticeable numbers begin to depart. How many made their back to Nova Scotia is debatable and will be considered later in this chapter. For present purposes, suffice it to say that the Acadians who were sent to Massachusetts were treated as some peculiar form of prisoners-of-war, although such a

---

57 24 January 1765, *Acts and Resolves ... Massachusetts Bay*, 6: 105.
58 "Jean Trahant, Castin Thibodet, Jean Hebaire, Charles Landry, Allexis Braux to the Governor and Commander in Chief of Massachusetts Bay, Boston 1st Jan. 1765," in *Report for 1905*, 2: App. E, 92–3.
59 Ibid., 96–9. See also *Act and Resolves ... Massachusetts Bay*, 4: 911.
60 Account published in Gaudet, "Acadian Genealogy," 100.

status was never officially accorded them. Since the majority of the Acadians had been born since 1713, on British territory, there was grave doubt as to what their legal rights might be. The question of subjecthood and citizenship is complex enough in the eighteenth century, whether the state be France, England, or a British North American colony. The rights of non-juring, native-born subjects posed a sufficient conundrum to colonial officials to make them cautious in their treatment of the Acadians. The Acadians were convinced that, if they were prisoners-of-war, then they should be treated as such: confined as a group, provided for by their enemy. If they were other than prisoners-of-war, then the limits placed on their freedom were utterly without justification. In either case, in Acadian eyes, forced separation of parents and children was monstrous. Massachusetts avoided any final pronouncement on the matter of Acadian legal status, referring to Acadians whenever possible as "inhabitants of Nova Scotia" or "exiles from Nova Scotia." The binding out of children, however, was halted. In the final analysis, however, whatever rights the Acadians might have had, their situation in Massachusetts was one of poverty, sickness, and limited freedom of movement. Their final disposition was as arbitrary as much of their treatment had been: a gradual and relatively unrecorded dispersal to destinations out of province.

From Massachusetts to Pennsylvania the governors, councils, and assemblies received the Acadians with considerable displeasure but made some sort of provision for their subsistence and something of an effort to keep them under surveillance until 1763. All these more northerly colonies attempted a distribution of the exiles among different towns and villages in order both to minimise the impact of the exiles on the public purse of any particular settlement and to prevent any conspiracy of the Acadians against their hosts. New York received some five hundred of the exiles and by 9 July 1756, had passed an act empowering the justices "to bind out such of his Majesty's Subjects, commonly called Neutral French ... to the End that they may not continue, as they now really are, useless to his Majesty, themselves and a burden on the Colony."[61] The justices were further urged to treat "the said people committed to their Care, with all the Justice in their Power, observing to make the most favourable contracts for them."[62]

61 W. Livingstone and W. Smith, eds., *Laws of New York from the 11th November, 1752 to 22nd of May, 1762*, 2 vols. (New York, 1762), 2: 103–4.
62 Ibid.

Connecticut received perhaps 400.[63] They were divided into groups of no more than seventeen persons, and usually of only six or seven, and the groups were distributed among fifty different settlements throughout that colony.[64] In 1760 there is a report that about twenty-two vessels arrived in Boston from Connecticut and were refused permission to land the Acadians they had on board.[65] The next destination of these Acadians would almost certainly have been Santo Domingo.

The history of the Acadians who went to the Caribbean is difficult to piece together. What is known at present can be summarized as follows. The Caribbean was, in every case, the exiles' second destination. In some cases, it was their third or fourth halt.[66] According to present knowledge, some 418 left from New York for Santo Domingo in 1764 and of these, 231 left in 1765 for Louisiana. In 1765, another 600 are reported as arriving in the Caribbean from "Acadie." It was thought they had been encouraged to do so by the English.[67] Parish registers indicate that the "Acadians were decimated by disease during the first months following their arrival".[68] What happened to them after that is a matter of debate. A large number went on to Louisiana, with either French or Spanish government aid. But there is no doubt that others remained, and in 1770 Acadians are still recorded in the records of Martinique, Guadaloupe, and Santo Domingo. In the mid-1820s a French government enquiry was undertaken for purposes of indemnifying former planters of Santo Domingo who had suffered losses during the Revolutionary year.[69]

63 Trumbell, James Hammond, and C.J. Hoadley, ed., *Public Records of the Colony of Connecticut, May, 1751–February, 1757* 15 vols. (New Haven, 1850–90), vol. 10.

64 "An Act for distributing and well-ordering the French people sent into this colony from Nova Scotia, January 1756," *Report for 1905*, 2: App. K, 254.

65 L.W. Cross, *The Acadians and the New England Planters* (Cambridge, NS, 1962).

66 J.T. Vocelle, *The Triumph of the Acadians* (1930), is the best short account but see also Gabriel Debien, "The Acadians in Santo Domingo," in Conrad, *The Cajuns*, 21–96.

67 Archives Colonial de Commerce de Guyenne, c. 4328, 1765, in 1F2161, AD, Ile-et-Vilaine (Rennes).

68 Debien, "The Acadians in Santo Domingo," in Conrad, *The Cajun*, 87.

69 *The Detailed List of Indemnities, Drawn up by the Commission Charged with Indemnifying the Former Planters of Santo Domingo, According to the Law of April 10th, 1826*, 6 vols. (Paris, 1827–33), cited in Conrad, *The Cajuns*, 90.

Only six Acadian names appear on this list.[70] In sum, the Acadians can be distinguished in the records of Santo Domingo from 1764 until 1790. After that date, information about them is sparse indeed.

To return to the experiences of the exiles in their places of first landing, the number sent directly to Pennsylvania does not seem to have been much more than that sent to New York and Connecticut. But the plight of the exiles seems to have produced much more concern among the legislators and leading men there than anywhere else except France. Approximately 400 Acadians were landed in Pennsylvania on December 1755.[71] The governor requested an immediate opinion of his council as to what should be done with them.[72] It was not until the spring of 1756 that Benjamin Franklin received the commission as the printer of the act for "dispersing the Inhabitants of Nova Scotia, imported into this Province, into the several Counties of Philadelphia."[73] The act made provisions much like those of Massachusetts, placing the Acadians in the hands of the overseers of the poor, but it added to the powers the command to settle the Acadians on farming families.[74] By January 1757, Pennsylvania had decided to follow the procedure of Massachusetts and bind out children, while continuing to make provision for the "aged, sick and maimed at the charge of the province."[75] The Acadians reacted as they had in Massachusetts: they wrote petitions saying that the law should be revoked. In one petition it was stated that "to separate innocent Children who have committed no Crime from their Parents appears contrary to the Precept of Jesus Christ."[76] This particular petition ended with the point that the Acadians should be permitted to depart as soon as they were able if they would give assurance that they would not join the French. "If we had inclined

---

70 A. Therior, Jacques Genton, Victoire Jourdain, Joseph Giroir, Michael Poirier, and Marie-Madeleine Poirier.

71 Samuel Hazard et al., eds., *Pennsylvania Archives: Selected and Arranged from the original documents in the Office of the Secretary of State of the Commonwealth* ... 138 vols. (Harrisburg and Philadelphia 3 PA, 1852–1935). Eight Series, 1931, 6: 4159.

72 "9th of December, 1755, Minutes of the Provincial Council, *Colonial Records, Pennsylvania*, 6: 751.

73 J.T. Mitchell and H. Flanders, eds., *Statutes at Large of Pennsylvania from 1682 to 1801*, 17 vols. (1896–1915), 5: 215–19.

74 Hazard et al., *Pennsylvania Archives*, 6: 4408.

75 Mitchell and Flanders, *Statutes at Large of Pennsylvania*, 278–80.

76 Public Archives of Pennsylvania, Votes of Assembly, 4509–12.

to War," they claimed, "we should have been still perhaps in our own Country."[77]

The records of the province show that binding out was halted and that the Acadians were supported "in great Measure by private Charities, whence they are become extremely burdensome to the well-disposed Inhabitants."[78] In 1760 an Acadian petition was sent to the Penn brothers in London, accompanied by a covering letter signed by several of Philadelphia's leading men. Pemberton, Hantin, Emton, and others wrote that the Acadians had been struck by all manner of diseases, but above all by smallpox. "Those who have survived," the letter continued, "have flattered themselves with a hope that at the End of the Warr, they should be restored to their former Possessions, which we conceive, arises in part from a Consciousness that they were dispossessed out of Political Considerations rather than by way of Punishment for any Offence."[79]

Pennsylvania records fall silent after this point until 1771 when an account was made of some twenty-two families still in Philadelphia, most of them burdened with sickness of one kind or another.[80] This account is very different from the contemporary accounts of the Acadians in Massachusetts during the 1760s, or from the comparable reports from France at the opening of 1770s, when officials in both places counted up to ten children a family. The Philadephia list is filled with details of the blind, of sick children, of children that were "Foolish." In general a picture is painted of the very depths of misery. Apart from the records of death, there is no clear indication in the archives of Pennsylvania whether the fate of those Acadians sent there led back to Nova Scotia or southward to the Caribbean and to Louisiana.

Maryland and colonies further south did not allow the Acadians complete freedom of movement, but the attempts of these colonies to circumscribe Acadian activities were less efficient and less long-lasting than the efforts of the more northerly colonies. As has been noted, the immediate response of Maryland to the Acadians was a mixture of fear and compassion, with fear predominating. The Act already cited, which banned them from witnessing any training manoeuvres, was followed five days later by an act to empower the

---

77 Ibid., 4512.
78 Hazard et al., *Pennsylvania Archives*, 6: 4901.
79 *"Pemberton Papers"* (Harrisburg, n.d.), 1: 99.
80 2 November 1771, Pennsylvania Historical Society Collections, printed in *American Catholic Historical Review* 18 (1901): 140–2.

justices of the county courts to make provision for the Acadians, who were to be dispersed through various settlements.[81] By 1757 various county supervisors were asking for help from the authorities at Annapolis. Talbot County commissioners reported that the Acadians "are become a grievance; inasmuch as we are not at present in a Situation and in a Circumstance capable of seconding their own Fruitless Endeavours to support their numerous families, as a People Plunder'd of their Effects: for tho' perhaps our Magistrates have taxed us, perhaps sufficient to feed such of them as cannot feed themselves, they cannot find Houses, Cloathing and other Comforts, in their Condition needful, without going from House to House Begging."[82]

By 1763 Maryland records show that about one-third of those landed in 1755 had died or emigrated.[83] In 1765 a petition by the Acadians was presented to the Justices of the Peace of Cecil County, asking for help to leave for the Mississippi.[84] Some ships did leave for this destination two years later. The *Maryland Gazette* reported that the schooner *Virgin* with some Acadians aboard cleared Annapolis in 1767.[85] But reports show that the passengers of this ship almost certainly ended up in Sante Fe.[86] The story of the Acadians sent to Maryland dwindles into the occasional genealogical detail and the fate of the majority becomes, once more, a matter for conjecture.

Once south of Maryland, the treatment meted out to the Acadians becomes even less uniform. As has been noted, Virginia exported the problem one more time. This colony introduced a bill into its House of Burgesses on 1 April 1756 to "enable certain persons to contract for the Transportation of the Neutral French to Great

---

81 27 May, 1756, *Proceedings and Acts of the General Assembly of Maryland* (Baltimore, 1930), 24: 542 ff.

82 Cited in B. Sollers, "The Acadians (French Neutrals) Transported to Maryland," *Maryland Historical Magazine* 3 (1907): 18.

83 "Census of Acadians, July 1763, photostat in Hall of Records, Annapolis, Maryland. The original is in the Archives Nationales (Paris), Affaires Etrangères, Politique Angleterre, vol. 451, f. 438.

84 Printed in J. Johnston, *History of Cecil County, Maryland* (Elkton, 1881), 263.

85 9 April 1767 (Annapolis).

86 B. Sollers, "Report on Smyth, *A Tour of U.S.A.* (London, 1784)," *Maryland Historical Magazine* 4 (1909): 279.

Britain."[87] The cost was about £5000.[88] North and South Carolina and Georgia kept less than total control of the exiles that came their way. North Carolina, in fact, had no Acadians actually destined for her shores. However, in Cape Few, on 22 April 1756, one Jacques Morris appeared: "on behalf of himself and one hundred French, being part of the French Neutrals sent to Georgia and come coastwise in small boats, having a pass for himself from Governor Reynolds [Georgia] and Governor Glen [South Carolina]."[89]

The exiles were allowed to continue north. There is considerable debate about whether any particular group that left a southern colony was the one which is reported as being held in custody in a more northerly jurisdiction. It is, however, probable that this group made it as far as New York.[90]

South Carolina received more than 1,000 Acadians.[91] The policy evolved in Charleston was a combination of the actions of Massachusetts, but with occasional forced labour, and the dispatch of a few families to England.[92] In general, however, exiles to this colony had their lives regulated by the legislation of 6 July 1756; this was entitled "An Act for disposing of the Acadians now in Charleston, by settling some fifth part of their number in the parishes of St. Philip and St. Michele and the four other parts of them in the other Parishes within this Province."[93] On 14 November 1755, Georgia received notice that Acadians had arrived. There was "great Confusion and Consternation"[94] and no coherent policy of any sort emerged from the discussions of governor and council. There were perhaps 600 to 700 Acadians in Savannah at any one time, and some of them were

87 McIlwaine, ed., *Journals of the Houses of Burgesses of Virginia* (Charlottesville, 1909), 353. The bill was given assent by the Governor on 15 April 1756.

88 "Governor Dinwiddie to Dobbs, June 11th, 1756," in Dinwiddie, *The Official Records*, 2: 442–3.

89 W. Saunders, *Colonial Records of North Carolina, 1752–59*, 5: 655.

90 Doughty, *The Acadian Exiles*, 147.

91 Figures derived from the reports of the arrival of various ships in *Carolina Gazette*, 13–20 November 20–27 November and 4–11 December 1755. See also C.J. Milling, *Exile without End* (Columbia, SC, 1945).

92 The best short account of this episode is Milling, *Exile without End*.

93 T. Cooper and David James Mac Cord, eds., *The Statutes at Large of South Carolina, 1682–1838*. 10 vols. (S. Carolina, 1836–41), 3: 31.

94 "Letter of Council to the Board of Trade, 5th January 1756," in Allan D. Candler, ed., *Colonial Records of the State of Georgia*, 7: 207.

provided with boats and allowed to attempt the journey back. Lawrence was writing indignantly to the Board of Trade in August 1756 that "French Inhabitants sent to Ga ... have been assisted at the Public Expense and are making for Nova Scotia."[95] Georgia did not manage to draft an act for "providing and disposing of the Acadians now in this province" until February 1757. At that point the provisions were similar to those of Massachusetts: the Acadians were divided among the townships and power was given to the Justices of the Peace to bind out the healthy into labour.[96]

The general impression one has of the deportation and years of exile is of the misery and distress of the Acadians. The entry for 8 October 1755 in Capt. Winslow's diary reads, "began to Embark the Inhabitants who went off Very Solentarily and unwillingly, the women in Great Distress Carrying off their children in their Arms, Others Carrying their Decript Parents in their Carts and all their Goods moving in Great Confusion and it appeared a scene of Woe and Distress."[97] His words are vivid and he is reporting a scene of human suffering accurately. But these words are utterly inadequate as a summary of Acadian reaction to what occurred. After all, the Acadians *survived* deportation and exile. Not only do some descendants of those loaded on the ships live as a coherent group in the Maritimes today, but others live as part of a coherent community which was established some 2,000 miles south. A 1930s survey of French-speaking peoples in the southern part of the state of Louisiana noted that "out of 120 families ... [there were] 108 reporting lines of descent on both sides as French ... 11 families reporting the use of both French and English in the home but French was the language stated to be most commonly used ... solidly Catholic in religion, not a single exception to be found ... [further] 72 of the families have as their nearest neighbour ... the family of a some relative ... [and this report] takes no account of relationships more remote than first cousin."[98]

The Acadians were nowhere merely passive recipients of the policies imposed on them by others. Even during the process of em-

---

95 Akins, *Nova Scotia Documents* 302–3.
96 *Statutes enacted by the Royal Legislature, Georgia* (1757), 18: 188.
97 "Winslow's Journals," *Collections of the Nova Scotia Historical Society*, 3: 166.
98 T.L. Smith, "An Analysis of Rural Social Organization Among the French Speaking People of Southern Louisiana," *Journal of Farm Economics* 16 (1937): 682–4.

barkation, some Acadian communities were able successfully to resist the plans for their exile. Once disembarked in new lands, the exiles continued to behave as if they were much more than just a body of refugees, or victims of war, and began to act with considerable political acumen. As soon as the Acadians had made even a minimal adaption to their new situation, they gathered their wits and wrote, or employed the local legal talent to write, petitions which set forth the totally unjustified nature of the punishment they had suffered and requested a variety of alterations in their situation.[99] This motif, that the deportation was basically unjust, is present no matter where the petitioners were and irrespective of whether the petition in question was made by an individual asking for consideration of a specific wrong, or by a group aimed at righting a more general wrong. Whether the petitions were written to the authorities of the British colonies in North America, to the British authorities in London by those Acadians sent abroad by Virginia, to the French authorities by the Acadians who arrived there between 1758 and 1764, or to the Spanish authorities at the time of the removal of Acadians from France to Louisiana in 1785, the tenor of the petitions is similar: for various and particular reasons, the deportation was unjustified and the authorities were asked to do something about the unfortunate situation in which the Acadians now found themselves.[100]

It is fascinating to compare the way in which this belief – that the deportation was a matter of singular injustice – was expressed to the different jurisdictions. In North America, of course, such petitions often contained assertions of past loyalty to British interests. For example, Joseph Michelle, in a protest sent to Governor Shirley of Massachusetts about the way in which his son was treated, remarked that he and his family had "been employed in repairing the forts at Annapolis, as an overseer of all Carts in bringing up Timber which I was obliged to do in the Night Time for fear of the Indians where I and my family run the risk of our Lives."[101] Similarly, in a handbill circulated in Philadelphia in 1758, the Acadians asserted

---

99 N.E.S. Griffiths, "Petitions of Acadian Exiles, 1755–1785. A Neglected Source," *Histoire Sociale / Social History* 11, no. 21 (mai–May 1978): 215–23 presents a summary of many of these.

100 A Selection of these petitions have been printed in *Report for 1905*, vol. 2; and L.H. Gipson, *The British Empire Before the American Revolution*, 6: chapter 6.

101 *Report for 1905, 2: App. E, 100.*

"Almost numberless are the Instances which might be given to the Abuses and Losses we have undergone from the French and the Indians, only on account of our adherence to our Oath of Fidelity."[102]

Those Acadians whose exile took them to England and to France also petitioned about the conditions under which they lived and the payment of the government support which both countries accorded them. In neither country were the Acadians over-awed by the status of those whose business it was to oversee their lives. The Acadians who arrived in England did so in early summer 1756. They are reported as numbering over 1,044.[103] They remained in England for nearly seven years and never hesitated to dispute measures that the British government took towards them. As peace approached in 1763, steps were taken to ask those Acadians then living in Liverpool, Southampton, Penryn, Falmouth, and Bristol what they hoped for. In no uncertain terms, the Acadians demanded that they be returned to Acadia. "We hope We shall be sent into Our Countries," their petition noted, "and that our Effects etc., which We have been dispossessed of (notwithstanding the faithful neutrality which We have always observed) will be restored to Us."[104] That these views were ignored does not alter the fact that those who expressed them had a clear idea of what their future should be. The immediate fate of these particular Acadians was to be shipped to France in the summer of 1763. They were fewer than the number that had arrived from Virginia, being in total no more than 866.[105]

These were by no means the first Acadians to arrive in France.[106] As early as 1749 an English vessel was reported as arriving at Nantes with "Acadians" from Louisbourg.[107] Almost ten years later, in 1758, separate arrivals were reported at Boulogne, Brest, Cherbourg, and St Malo; in 1759, further listings are given for ships arriving at Boulogne, Dunkerque, and St Malo; in 1760 there is a listing for Cher-

102 Hazard et al., *Pennsylvania Archives, First Series, 1752–1756*, 3: 566.
103 N.E.S. Griffiths, "Acadians in Exile," *Acadiensis* 4 (1974): 70.
104 "L.G. and J.B. to John Cleveland, 4th January, 1763, Admiralty Records 98/9," partially printed in ibid., 74.
105 *Report for 1905*, 2: 150.
106 For a general survey of Acadian experience in France see N.E.S. Griffiths, "The Acadians Who Returned to France," *Natural History* 90 (1981): 48–57.
107 There is not much information about these people, save that they are called Acadian in the port listings of arrival, 1F2160, Archives d'Ille-et-Vilaine (Rennes).

bourg; in 1761 for Rochefort; and in 1763 for Marlaix. [108] The numbers are difficult to establish. I would estimate that, including those sent on from England, there were some 3,000 Acadians in France at the end of 1763.

Their attitude towards French officialdom was as trenchant as it had been to English bureaucracy. The first reply of the exiles to French proposals for their settlement in Belle-Ile-en-Mer, a small island off the south coast of Brittany, was less than grateful. In the Acadians' view, the land was poor, and the island far too near English power for comfort. [109] This response set the tone for much of the future interaction between the Acadians and French authorities. The two major attempts at resettlement, at Belle Ile and at "La ligne acadienne" in Poitou, both failed. [110] The majority of the Acadians left France in 1785 for Louisiana. [111]

At first sight, this seems surprising. Acadians were, after all, French-speaking Catholics: there was at least a supposition of commonalty of interest with the French nation, and one of the proposed sites for their resettlement was in a part of France from which many of their ancestors had emigrated. Superficially, having been given considerable aid from the French government and having had the experience of exile in British communities, assimilation into eighteenth-century France would appear a distinct possibility. But this did not happen: the Acadians were French-speaking and Catholic, but they were also North American. The norms of the Acadians during the twenty years they spent in France were dominated by the Acadian identity that had been forged in "Acadia or Nova Scotia." They did not prove malleable to French influence. Some reasons for this are suggested in a letter by a lawyer of Dinan in 1759 to the naval commissioner at St Malo, asking help for the

---

108 Ibid.
109 "Petition dated Morlaix, 31sr 8bre 1763, c. 5058, AD, Ile-et-Vilaine, (Rennes).
110 Winzerling, *Acadian Odyssey*, describes the arrival in France of those who had been sent to England. The works of Milton P. Rieder and Norma Gaudet Rieder, including *The Acadians in France*, 3 vols. (Lafayette, 1973), are most useful. Ernest Martin, *Les exiles Acadiens en France au xviii siècle et leur établissement en Poitou* (Brissard, 1979) gives a solid narrative of Acadian experience in one area of France from 1763 to 1785.
111 N.E.S. Griffiths, "Les Acadiens et leur établissement en Louisiane," *France-Amérique* 35 (1983): 1–4.

twenty-two Acadians he had established on his own farm.[112] He wrote in part as follows: "Premierement ses peuples sont elévés dans un pays d'abondance, de terres a discretion, par consequent moins difficile a cultiver ... de plus les hommes ... ressentent déjà les chaleurs quoy aye point encore sensibles pour nous, ils mannient un peu la hache pour logement et assez mal quelques chose a leurs usages, ce qu'on n'appeller que hacheur des bois, les femmes filent un peu des bas." According to this same source, the Acadians wanted a great deal of bread, demanded milk and butter, and would not be weaned to cider: the desire for North American foodstuffs had replaced an appetite for French staples.

But material customs, however, are only a part – if an important part – of the life of a distinct community. The Acadians confronted not merely a different agricultural environment but a fundamentally different social and political context. As was shown very early on in the Belle Ile experiment, the Acadians were not used to the structured organization of eighteenth-century French bureaucracy.[113] Acadians did not like tithes, bitterly resented the idea that they should stay in one place, and found little in common with their new neighbours, the original inhabitants of Belle Ile. Similarly, the efforts made in the 1770s to establish the Acadians on the estates of the Marquis de Perusse des Cars came to naught.[114] Although one can find traces that record the treatment of Acadians as a distinct group in France as late as 1828, after 1785 their history there is once again a matter of genealogical interest in individuals rather than a question of the survival of a community.

The reactions of a group in exile are influenced not only by conditions existing within the group but also by their new external environment. The binding nature of Acadian kinship ties was reinforced by their total lack of such ties, at least during the early years, with the people among whom they were exiled. The Acadians retained their identity in exile partly because of official policies that designated them a group. Thus, the ways in which governments organized the exiles, paid them pensions, or settled them in areas reserved exclusively for them all helped preserve the Acadian sense of their unique identity. But when all is said and done, the Acadians remained a coherent group in exile because they were a coherent

---

112 "Dinan, l'avocat de la Crochais to Guilot, St. Malo, 10 mai 1750," IF2159, Archives d'Ille-et-Vilaine, Rennes.
113 Griffiths "The Acadians Who Returned to France," 53 ff.
114 On this see Martin, *Les exiles Acadiens*.

people before they went into exile. It is the sense of community that was part and parcel of the Acadians as individuals that led to behaviour which caused a Georgia official to comment, "such is the Bigotry and Obstinacy of these People that they have chosen rather to live miserably than to separate and live comfortably."[115]

The most important resources that the Acadians took with them into exile were social and political strengths. Acadian society was really built on the extended family. Thus, while brutal family separations did take place during the exile, there always remained a web of family linkages which supported the individuals in the strange new lands. The network of inter-marriages, which brought together people from different settlements as well as from within the same village, is documented in the registers compiled by the French government for Belle Ile.[116] The psychological impact of the trauma, the impact of death and sickness, would be somewhat mitigated by the presence of people who were obviously kin. The political experience of the Acadians before 1755 gave the exiles not only a known pattern of leadership, but forged a people accustomed to arguing with an authority that, in its own eyes, was stronger and more righteous.

There was a third factor which not only sustained the Acadians who went into exile but was also a significant factor in the continuance of the Acadians in Nova Scotia. This was the belief, held by the community as a whole, that the Acadians were a people distinct from others. Their legitimate country was "Acadia or Nova Scotia." The eighteenth century Acadians were not a nation, but they were a distinct culture. The Acadian sense that the lands surrounding their villages were theirs to exploit, coupled with a clear sense of the family connections which ran from village to village and a distinctive life-style, was by 1755 the fundamental background for Acadian political action. The Acadians considered that they had developed a political culture which fitted the needs of the society that they had built between two empires. In the Acadian view, a view that is repeated over and over again in the petitions they presented in exile, they had done nothing, nothing at all, to deserve

---

115 "Report of the Committee ... 12th July, 1760" in the Journals of the House of Assembly, State Archives, Columbia, South Carolina. These records are now part of a publication series, viz: Easterby, J.H., ed., *The Journal of the Commons House of assembly of South Carolina, South Carolina colonial Records*.

116 Rieder and Rieder, eds., *The Acadians in France*, vol. 2.

deportation. It is the sense of being a society, of possessing both a group identity and the right to live in a particular place, that allowed the Acadians to surmount the exile and later rebuild their community in the Maritimes, as well as establishing another in Louisiana.

The deportation was not an incident which took place in a single year, but a policy pursued until 1763. Despite the zeal with which the policy was prosecuted, however, the colony was never entirely without Acadians.[117] On 16 July 1764, the Lords of Trade informed the governor of Nova Scotia that he should allow the Acadians to settle in Nova Scotia, provided they took the oath of allegiance, in spite of their "having taken up Arms in support of France during the late war."[118] Nine years after the transports first left, the Acadians were admitted once more as subjects with legal status in the colony. There were at that time about 1,500 of them actually within Nova Scotia.[119]

From the moment they left the coast of Nova Scotia, the Acadians had made every effort to return. Even those who escaped to Quebec did not find that society to their liking. Bishop Pontbriand wrote in 1756 that "le sort des Acadiens m'afflige; a en juger par ceux qui sont ici, ils ne veulent par demeurer parmi nous."[120] They returned from all points of the globe, Massachusetts as well as France. On arrival in Nova Scotia they found their former lands occupied, their villages truly conquered territory. They found that those who had escaped deportation had relocated in new settlements, some within the peninsula but most on the very boundaries of the territory once called "Acadia or Nova Scotia." They had some choice. They could attach themselves to the Acadian communities within Nova Scotia on the lands which had been specifically assigned to them: in particular, they could join those living along Baie St Marie, district of Clare.[121] They could elect to join the tiny communities on Cape Breton Island or to join those established in what after 1798 would be called Prince Edward Island. They could go to the Acadian communities that existed in what would become New Brunswick in 1784,

117 *Censuses of Canada, 1665–1871* (Ottawa, 1876), 4: xxviii.

118 "Lords of Trade to Wilmot, July 16th, 1764," NA, CO 218/6, B 1115.

119 PANS, "Early Descriptions of Nova Scotia," *Reports* (Halifax, 1943), App. B, part 2, 32.

120 "Pontbriand a Belair, 23rd juillet, 1756," Archives Archévêque de Québec, (Quebec), 2: 620.

121 M.A. Tremblay, "Les Acadiens de la Baie Francaise: L'histoire d'une survivance," *Revue de l'histoire de l'Amerique francaise* 20 (1962).

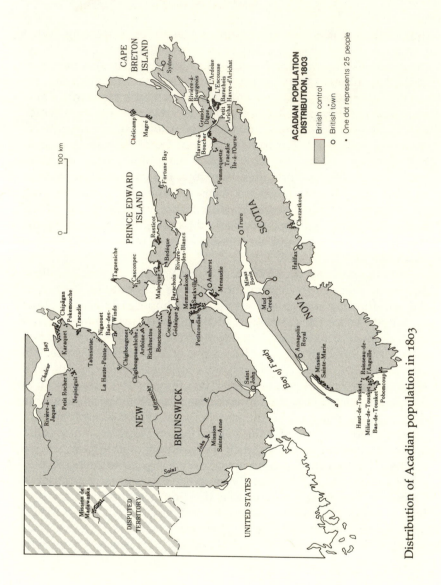

ACADIAN POPULATION DISTRIBUTION, 1803

British control

○ British town

• One dot represents 25 people

0   100 km

CAPE BRETON ISLAND

Sydney

Rivière-à-Bourgeois

L'Ardoise

L'Escousse

Grande Digue

Petit Barachois

Tracadie

Havre-d'Arichat

Arichat

Havre-à-Boucher

Pommequette

Tracadie

Île-à-l'Ourse

Chéticamp

Magré

Fortune Bay

PRINCE EDWARD ISLAND

Tagueniche

Rustico

Cascompec

Bedéque

Rivière-des-Blancs

Malpèque

Barachois

Menaudie

Amherst

Sackville

Memramkook

Cocagne

Gédaïque

Petitcoudiac

Coaque-

Ardoine

Richibouctou

Nigaouet

Baie-des-Winds

Chigbougouachiche

Chugbougonet

La Haute-Pointe

Tabusintac

Nepisiqui

Petit Rochers

Rivière-à-Jaquet

Chipāgan

Karaquet

Pokemouche

Tracadie

Chaleur Bay

NEW BRUNSWICK

Memramkook R.

Saint John R.

Saint John

Mission Sainte-Anne

Mission de Madawaska

DISPUTED TERRITORY

UNITED STATES

Bay of Fundy

Truro

SCOTIA

Chezzetkouk

Halifax

Minas Basin

Mud Creek

Annapolis Royal

NOVA

Mission Sainte-Marie

Haut-de-Tousket

Milieu-de-Tousket

Bas-de-Tousket

Ruisseau-de-l'Anguille

Pobomcoup

Distribution of Acadian population in 1803

either to those of the St John River Valley or to those on its coast between the Baie de Chaleurs and Baie Verte.

Wherever the Acadians were established after 1764, one thing became clear: their sense of themselves as a people was undiminished. As far as it lay in their power, they attempted to recreate the same self-contained and independent life they had had before 1755. The circumstances were very different. They were no longer a border people but were now merely one group within a large empire. By the end of the 1780s, the Acadians had recovered some of their former demographic strength, but they were still a minority in the three Maritime colonies and would remain so over the ensuing decades. Yet the reports sent by Quebec missionaries to the Archbishop of Quebec in the late 1780s still characterize the Acadians as stubborn, argumentative, and clearly determined to assert their right to argue the politics of their lives with all those who considered them subject to their authority.[122] The subsequent growth and development of the identity of this Acadian society is as complex as the history of its genesis. It was an identity that included not only the experience of the cataclysmic events of the Deportation but also beliefs about the pre-deportation Acadian society. It was an identity that would be built not only on a common language and religion, and on a common culture, but on a common interpretation of the history of the Deportation. The Acadians of the nineteenth century would find an extraordinary force for unity in their adherence to a particular interpretation of the events of 1755. One thing is clear, the policy initiated by Colonel Lawrence at mid-century failed to destroy the Acadian community. Further, in the very circumstances of its failure, it provided the Acadians with one of the foundations of their unique identity in the centuries to come.

122 "Etat de la Mission de l'Acadie," Archives Archévêque de Québec
NE/1–12, 1786.

Conclusion

The theme of Acadian history that is central to this monograph is that of the creation and endurance of a people. It is the common thread that links the four epochs of Acadian history outlined: 1686–89 and the achievement of a European settlement on the territory claimed; 1729–30 and the establishment of the identity of a new community; 1748–55 when the political strength of the new community proved insufficient to prevent its devastation; and 1755–84, when it became clear that the work of five generations was strong enough to be the foundation of a continuing group identity.

As the twentieth century draws to a close, many a scholar – sociologist and psychologist, political scientist and economist, even the historian – has been startled to find that communities cling to and fight for beliefs about culture and identity that a generation ago appeared to be losing strength.[1] The endurance of minority "national" identities has become of greater and greater interest as the tension between individuals of various cultural heritages creates immediate problems within the old nation states. Whether it is Scottish separatism or the demands of the Basque, the requests for the use of Spanish in Florida and Texas schools or statements of the Lithuanian parliament, the platform of the CoR party or the language bills of Quebec – all confirm that the problem Gellner has

---

1 References here could be of inordinate length. My own thinking on this subject has been much influenced by Philip K. Bock, *Rethinking Psychological Anthropology: Continuity and Change in the Study of Human Action* (New York, 1988); Ernest Gellner, *Culture, Identity and Politics* (Cambridge, 1987); and Lynn Hunt, ed., *The New Cultural History* (California, 1989).

labelled "nationalism and cohesion in complex societies" is indeed a major issue in late-twentieth-century life. Most attempts to understand the issue work from the idea of the state as the pinnacle of national achievement, without which, indeed, some assert no "nation" can be called mature. The importance and the more obvious power of the collective is often seen as the best place to comprehend the phenomenon. The reality of the individual experience and its importance to the collectivity is a matter that has been less often examined. It is the methodologies of sociology, political science, and economics that have been most fully exploited in the quest for an understanding of the phenomena of nationalism.

Yet the understanding of the statistical norms of a community is an understanding of only part of the human experience. The enquiry into the systems by which a community organizes its functions is an enquiry about only one part of human life. Even what Stoianovich has summarized as the *Annales* paradigm – an enquiry "as to how the whole collectivity functions in terms of its multiple temporal, spatial, human, social, economic, cultural and environmental dimensions"[2] – still contains only part of the complexity of human life. In the final analysis, there remains the matter of the action of the individual, the sense a single person makes of existence, the variation from the average that characterizes the personal and the private. The collectivity is, after all, precisely that: a bringing together of individuals.[3] There has to be some examination of the link between the components – the individual whose particular characteristics have been summarized and the people described, the people created.

My own ambition in writing about Acadian history has been, and is, to tackle the problem first from the most simple human level: why and how did individuals with very separate and different heritages band into the specific Acadian community? What sorts of individual strengths enabled that community to survive? I am attempting to find "the middle ground of human participation and

2 Traian Stoainovich, *French Historical Method: The Annales Paradigm* (Ithaca, 1976), 236.

3 As Donald Kelley wrote: "The dilemma ... is the old problem of universals – or the newer one of statistical conformity – and if it is ultimately insoluble, the historian is bound sometimes to make the attempt." *The Beginning of Ideology Consciousness and Society in the French Reformation* (Cambridge, 1981), 8.

reaction to society, ground which is properly that of the historian, inaccessible as it may seem methodologically."[4]

As I acknowledged in the "Introduction," it is a considerable ambition. In the furtherance of this ambition, the space of time which Mount Allison University conferred upon me when I was awarded the Chair of Maritime Studies has proved both a blessing and a salutary warning. It is a blessing in that it has allowed me to prepare this monograph, which is something in the nature of a blueprint for the larger work on which I am engaged: that of an analytical narrative of Acadian history from 1604 to 1784. It has proved a warning at the same time because it has made me very conscious of a raft of questions that have received scant attention in the previous chapters and must be placed somewhere in the larger work. The most important relate to the lives of those Acadians who were women, to the extraordinary impact of the Micmac upon the Acadian community, and to the strength of Acadian culture, both material and in the form of artistic endeavour.

Let me conclude with the words of a poet to convey something of why I try to understand Acadian history:

it is the dead who sing. who is
to match their great chorus? I
bend to them in this graveyard at
Jolicure. only the flag on my
friend's plot waves. there is the
murmur of his voice. word after
word. there is no forgetting John.
whatever tack I take[5]

There is no forgetting Acadia for me, whether I live close to the shores of her birth or in some distand land.

4 Ibid.
5 Douglas Lochhead, *High Marsh Road* (Toronto, 1980), n.p. [lines for a diary, 27 November].

Bibliographic Notes

The footnotes show those sources most relied on for these essays. However, those interested in further reading on the Acadians will find the following notes useful. It should be borne in mind that this list is meant to indicate only a very few of the works available on topics relating to Acadian history.

1   The sources for Acadian history, both primary and secondary, are rich and various. The best introduction to them is the work by the Centre d'études acadiennes, Université de Moncton. In 1975 the Centre published the first volume of an *Inventaire general des sources documentaires sur les Acadiens*. This was followed by a *Bibliographie Acadienne liste de volumes et thèses concernant l'Acadie et les Acadiens dès debuts à 1975* (n.d.). In 1988 a third volume appeared entitled *Guide bibliographique de l'Acadie 1976–1987*. As well as revealing the extent of material available for studying Acadian history, these works also demonstrate the extent to which much of it is to be found at the Centre d'études acadiennes. Microfilm, microfiche, photocopies – all the late twentieth-century facsimile aids for the reproduction of documents have been employed to ensure that the collection of Acadiana there is both as wide-ranging and exhaustive as funds and scholarly endeavour allow.

2   In considering the international aspect of Acadian history, a good starting place for French history is Fernand Braudel, *The Identity of France*, vol. 1., *History and Environment* (London, 1988). For England see J.R. Jones, *Country and Court England, 1658–1714* (London, 1978). The best sources for colonial British America are voluminous and the reader is urged to consult Jack P. Greene and J.R. Pole, eds., *Colonial British America: Essays in the New History of the Early Modern Era* (Baltimore, 1984).

3   For the history of the Micmacs, W.D. Wallis and S. Wallis, *The Micmac Indians of Eastern Canada* (Minneapolis, 1955) is indispensable. But see also

Philip K. Bock, "Micmac" in Bruce Trigger, ed., *Handbook of North American Indians*, vol. 15, Northeast (Washington, 1978). A.G. Bailey, *The Conflict of European and Eastern Algonkian Cultures, 1504–1700*, 2nd. ed. (Toronto, 1969) is a classic study of contact between Micmac and European. See also Cornelius J. Jaenen, "Friend and Foe: Aspects of French-Amerindian Cultural Contacts in the Sixteenth and Seventeenth Century," *Canadian Historical Review* 55 (1974): 261–99. A controversial interpretation of the subject is to be found in Calvin Martin, *Keepers of the Game* (Berkeley, 1978).

4   Monographs of particular interest in Acadian history are:

J.B. Brebner, *New England's Outpost: Acadia Before the Conquest of Canada* (New York, 1927). This is the classic study of Acadia as a British colony.

Glenn Conrad, ed., *The Cajuns: Essays on Their History and Culture* (Louisiana, 1978). This is the best single collection of essays on the Acadians in Louisiana.

John G. Reid, *Acadia, Maine and New Scotland: Marginal Colonies in the Seventeenth Century* (Toronto, 1981). This study places early Acadian history in the context of the European settlement of the area.

Andrew Hill Clark, *Acadia: The Geography of Early Nova Scotia to 1760* (Madison, 1968). This is a fine study of the historical geography of "Acadia or Nova Scotia."

Jean Daigle, ed., *The Acadians of the Maritimes: Thematic Studies* (Moncton, 1982). This is the translation of a work published in French in 1980. The essays present the views and ideas of contemporary Francophone scholars about Acadian history and society. It is excellent.

Geneviève Massignon, *Les parlers francais d'Acadie* (Paris, 1955). This two-volume work is much more than a collection of the speech patterns of the Acadians; it is an exhaustive analysis of the historical roots of the Acadian language.

George A. Rawlyk, *Nova Scotia's Massachusetts: A Study of Massachusetts–Nova Scotia Relationships, 1630–1784* (Montreal, 1974). This good work was the first to modify the ideas put forward by Brebner on the impact of Massachusetts on Acadia.

John G. Reid, *Six Crucial Decades: Times of Change in the History of the Maritimes* (Halifax, 1987). This work is a series of essays, and the one on the "1750's: Decade of Expulsion" is brilliant in conceptualizing Acadian history.

G.F.G. Stanley, *New France: The Last Phase* (Toronto, 1969). This provides a clear account of the international arguments over Acadia at the critical time of the deportation.

5   Works which present some viewpoints of the contemporary Acadian community include Michel Roy, *L'Acadie des origines à nos jours: Essai de synthèse historique* (Quebec, 1981); and Leon Theriault, *La question du pouvoir en Acadia* (Moncton, 1982).

Index